The Negro Travelers' Green Book

1954 Facsimile Edition

Victor H. Green

© Copyright 2017 by Snowball Publishing
Published by Victor H. Green

www.snowballpublishing.com

info@snowballpublishing.com

For information regarding special discounts for bulk purchases, please contact
Snowball Publishing at

sale@snowballpublishing.com

A Chat With The Editor

TRAVELING is one of the large industries of this era. Millions of people hit the road as soon as the warm weather sets in. They want to get away from their old surroundings: to see—to learn how people live—to meet old and new friends.

In this era of the automobile, trains, buses, boats and fast flying air liners, we have an assortment of transportation which will take one to any place that they might wish to go. With all of these transportation facilities at hand, modern travel has brought thousands of people out of their homes to view the wonders of the world.

Thousands and thousands of dollars are spent each year in the various modes of transportation. Money spent like this brings added revenue to trades people throughout the country.

The white traveler for years has had no difficulty in getting accomodations, but with the Negro it has been different. He before the advent of Negro Travel Guides has had to depend on word of mouth and then sometimes accommodations weren't available. But now a days things are different—he has his own travel guide, that he can depend on for all the information that he wants and with a selection. Hence these guides have made traveling more popular and without running into embarrassing situations.

Since 1936, THE GREEN BOOK has been published yearly. A few years after its publication, THE GREEN BOOK was recognized as the official Negro Travel Guide by the United States Travel Bureau, a part of the Department of Commerce, which bureau has been closed, due to the lack of funds. By being such an important piece of literature, white business has also recognized its value and it is now in use by the Esso Standard Oil Co., The American Automobile Assn. and its affiliate automobile clubs throughout the country, other automobile clubs, air lines, travel bureaus, travelers aid, libraries and thousands of subscribers.

Hence we have filled one of our life's ambitions, to give the Negro a travel guide that will be of service to him, by this method we have established ourselves in the minds of the traveling public. THE GREEN BOOK is known from coast to coast as the source of information for travel and vacations.

VICTOR H. GREEN,
Editor & Publisher

THE NEGRO TRAVELERS' GREEN BOOK

The Guide to Travel and Vacations

VICTOR H. GREEN, Editor & Publisher

IN THIS ISSUE

INDEX

THE NEGRO TRAVELERS' GREEN BOOK, published yearly by Victor H. Green & Co., 200 West 135th St., New York 30, N. Y. ADVERTISING RATES, write to the publishers, last forms close Dec. 1. We reserve the right to reject any advertising which does not conform to our standards. SUBSCRIPTIONS: Prices in the United States, $1.25 post paid; Foreign (Outside the U. S.) $1.50 in advance. RUSH ORDERS: send 9c, first class; air mail, 18c; Special delivery, 29c. Copyrighted 1953 by Victor H. Green.

Dreams or Problems Worry You? Send in Your Dream
or Problem Today!

Prof. Diamond's {DREAM} Formula

Opportunity . . .

At Last It's Here!

A Sure Way!

Respect Your
Dreams. They
May Mean
Wealth
Success
Happiness

INTRODUCTION

For many years men have traveled all over the world trying to find an accurate method of analyzing life's DREAMS and PROBLEMS. Unfortunately, few have succeeded in discovering the secrets of DREAMS and the PROBLEMS of life.

Not only do I analyze your DREAM, which guides your every move in life, but I also solve your PROBLEMS by use of the AMAZING DREAM FORMULA. We have helped thousands with their DREAMS and PROBLEMS.

Mail in your DREAM or PROBLEM together with $1.00 to Prof. DIAMOND P. O. Box 172, G. P. O. New York 1, N. Y. When you mail in your DREAM or PROBLEM, you automatically become a member of the DIAMOND DREAM CLUB, which entitles you to many FREE benefits. The DREAM FORMULA will not fail you.

Send in for information regarding Prof. DIAMOND'S DREAM CHART, which reveals the secret numbers you live under, as compounded by the DIAMOND DREAM FORMULA.

Distributed and Copyrighted 1949 by Prof. Diamond, P.O. Box 172, G.P.O., N.Y.C.

PHOTO CREDITS: First & fourth covers, also pages 12, 13, 15, 16, 17 by courtesy of The Californians, Inc., San Francisco, California.

U. S. BOND'S MOTEL, MADISON, ARKANSAS

On Highway 70, 40 miles west of Memphis, Tennessee, 100 miles East of Little Rock, Ark., ½ mile west of Madison, Arkansas. Strictly Modern baths, Beauty Rest mattresses, built-in wall furnaces air-conditioned and ventilated fans. Room service, Meals served in rooms. Phone No. 133JI1

The South's finest and one of America's best Motels for Colored. Garages in rear.

4

The Green Book
Motel Guide

We herewith supply you with these listings of Colored and White Motel owners throughout the United States. They are all first class motels and desire your patronage. Each place has been contacted. If in applying for accommodations you are refused, kindly notify us about same, giving us the reasons, we shall contact this particular place and remove their listing. DON'T BE DISAPPOINTED—make advance reservations. State date of arrival, number of persons in your party—adults or children and number of single or double beds required. After confirmation of reservation, send one nights lodging to be certain reservations will be held.

ARKANSAS

HOT SPRINGS
McKenzie Unique, 301 Henry St.
MADISON
Bond's, Rt. 70 1/" Mile West
of Madison (see ad. opposite page)

ARIZONA

KINGMAN
White Rock, Rt. 66, East end
of Town

CALIFORNIA

LOS ANGELES
Roberson's, 2111 E. Imperial Blvd
Johnson's, 1186 So. Wilmington
Western, Cor. W. 37th St. &
Western Ave.
Thomas, 2050 W. Jefferson Blvd.
Haye's, 960 E. Jefferson Blvd.
NEEDLES
El Adobe, Rt. 66

COLORADO

MONTROSE
Davis Auto Court

CONNECTICUT

POMFRET
The Willow Inn, Rt. 44, ½ Mile
West of Conn. Rt. 101 &
U. S. 44

DELAWARE

REHOBOTH BEACH
Mallory Cabins, Phone 8991
Rehoboth Ave. Ext.

FLORIDA

FERNANDINA
American Beach
JACKSONVILLE
A. L. Lewis, P. O. Box 660
OCALA
Carmen Manor Hotel
1044 W. Broadway St.

EBONY MOTEL

Kings Road at Cleveland St.

New, Modern - Air Conditioned
Steam Heat - Private Bath
*Located near Railway and Bus Stations,
Amusements, Business*
On Highway No. 1
REASONABLE RATES
JACKSONVILLE, FLA.

I O W A
CEDAR RAPIDS

MOTEL SEPIA

CECIL & EVELYN REED, Props.
Clean, Modern, Air Conditioned
On Coast to Coast Highways 30 & 150
3 Miles East of Cedar Rapids
CEDAR RAPIDS, IOWA
Phone: 9736 or 3-8881

5

ILLINOIS
FULTON
Twin Oaks, Rt. 30, 4 Miles
east of Fulton

INDIANA
FURNESSVILLE
Roby's Country Club, Rt. 20
GARY
Roby's Country Club
20 miles N. E. of Gary

NEVADA
ELKO
Louis Motel
2Miles West of Elko

OKLAHOMA
TULSA
Avalon Motel
2411-13 E. Aapache St.
Phone: 6-2572

PENNSYLVANIA
WASHINGTON
Motel Todd,
12½ Linn Avenue
Phone 4972
POTTSTOWN
Cedar Haven, Pa. Rt. 422, bet.
Reading & Pottstown

TEXAS

MARSHALL
La Casa Motel, Route 5, Box 32
La Casa, Rt. 80, 2 Miles West
TEXARKANA
Sunset, 1568 North St.
SAN ANTONIO
Ritz Motel & Coffee Shop
2958 E. Commerce
Phone: Circle 4-6607

KANSAS
BOGUE
Tourist Court, Junction Rt. U. S. 24
STOCKTON
L. D. Fuller

MAINE
ROBBINSTON
Brook's Bluff Cottage, Rt. 1,
12 Miles E. of Calais
DIXFIELD
Marigold Cabins, Rt. 2 10 Miles
East of Rumford

MASSACHUSETTS
TRAILER PARK
Mrs. Mary B. Pina, 26 Heed St.
WAREHAM
Mrs. L. Anderson, 294 Elm St.

MICHIGAN
VANDALIA
Copper, Rt. M 60, bet. Chicago
& Detroit

NEW JERSEY
SOUTH PLEASANTVILLE
Fuller's, Rt. 9, Rt. 4
ASBURY PARK
Waverley, 138 DeWitt Ave.

NEW YORK STATE
ALBANY
White Birch Motel, Rt. 9, 15
Miles N. of Albany

NEW HAMPSHIRE
RUMNEY DEPOT
Whispering Pines, Rt. 25, 8 Miles
North of Plymouth

NEW MEXICO
VADO
Fuller's, 3 N 1, Highway 80

LORDSBURG

NORTH CAROLINA

HAMLET
C. B. Covington, North Yard

SOUTH CAROLINA

MYRTLE BEACH
MOTOR COURT
Fitzgerald's, Carver St.
Charles' Place
DARLINGTON
Mable's Motel

SOUTH DAKOTA

CUSTER
Rocket Court, 211 Custer Ave. on
U. S. Rt. 16 & 85
WATERTOWN
5th Ave. & 212 Motel, U. S. Rt. 212

VIRGINIA

PETERSBURG
Lord Nelson, Rts. 1 & 301, bet.
Petersburg & Richmond

ROANOKE
Pine Oak Inn, Rt. 460
Bet. Salem & Roanoke

WEST VIRGINIA

CHARLESTON
Hall's Park, U. S. Rt. 60
West of Charleston

EXPLANATION

No travel Guide is perfect! The changing conditions as all know, contribute to this condition, particularly in the United States.

The listings in this Guide are carefully checked and, despite this, past experiences have shown that our minute inspection had failed to notice errors which would be an inconvenience to the traveler. Therefore, at this point may we emphasize that these listings are printed just as they are presented to us and we would like your cooperation and understanding, that the publishers are not responsible for miscalculations or errors after this check has been made.

We appreciate letters from you, our patrons, donating advice and addresses of places not listed herein, that would be in accord with our level. We also welcome adverse criticism, in that, it might improve our standards, and, in the end, afford more comfortable conditions for you and others.

This Guide Book is not sold on newsstands but in bookstores. They make appreciative gifts to friends and neighbors. Inasmuch as the sale of these Guide Books depend mostly upon the friend-to-friend oral advertising system, it would be particularly interesting if more of our patrons would pass the word along concerning our "Green Book."

For further information concerning this matter you may contact our agents or the publishers: Victor H. Green & Co., 200 West 135th St., Room 215A, New York 30, N. Y.

ALABAMA

BIRMINGHAM
HOTELS
Dunbar , 323 N. 17th St.
Fraternal, 1614 4th Ave. N.
Palm Leaf, 328½ N. 18th St.
New Home, 1718½ 4th Ave.

GADSDEN
TOURISTS HOMES
Mrs. A. Sheperd, 1324 4th Ave.
Mrs. J. Simons, 233 N. 6th St.

MOBILE
HOTELS
Blue Heaven, 361 Morton St.
TOURISTS HOMES
Midway Traders, 107 N. Dearborn
E. Reed, 950 Lyons St.
E. Jordan, 256 N. Dearborn St.
F. Wildins 254 N. Dearborn St.

MONTGOMERY
HOTELS
Hotel Ben Moore
Cor. High & Jackson Sts.
Ben Moore, Cor. High & Jackson
Douglass, 121 Monroe Ave.
TAVERNS
Douglas, 121 Monroe Ave.

SHEFFIELD
HOTELS
McClain, 19th St.
TOURISTS HOMES
Mrs. Mattie Herron, 1003 E. 19th St.

TUSCALOOSA
TOURISTS HOMES
Mrs. Clopton, 1516 25th Ave.

ARIZONA

DOUGLAS
TOURIST HOMES
Faustina Wilson, 1002 16th St.

NOGALES
RESTAURANTS
Bell's Cafe. 325 Morley Ave.

PHOENIX
HOTELS
Paducah Hotel
14 No. 6th Street
Winston Inn
1342 E. Jefferson St.
TOURIST HOMES
Swindall's Tourist Home
1021 E. Washington St.
Louis Jordan, 2118 Violet Dr. E.
Mrs. L. Stewart, 1134 E. Jefferson

Gardener's, 1229 E. Washington St.
Mrs. Bea. Jackson, 811 E. Monroe
RESTAURANTS
Alhambia, 1246-48 E. Wash. St.
Jefferson, 1303 E. Jefferson St.
Tapp's, 209 W. Hadley St.
Rose, 947 W. Watkins Rd.
BEAUTY PARLORS
Thelma's, 33 So. 1st Ave.
C. Jackson, 1238 E. Madison St.
BARBER SHOPS
Hagler's, 345 E. Jefferson
Bryant's, 620 S. 7th Ave.
TAVERNS
Vaughn's, 1248 E. Washington Ave.
SERVICE STATIONS
Super, 1245 Washington St.
GARAGES
DRUG STORES
Johnson's, 1140 E. Washington St.
LIQUOR STORES
Broadway, 1606 East Broadway

TUCSON
TOURIST HOMES
Mrs. Louise Pitts, 722 N. Perry St.

YUMA
HOTELS
Brown's, 196 N. Main St.
TOURIST HOMES
Mrs. John A. Gordon, 192 N. 5th

ARKANSAS

ARKADELPHIA
HOTELS
Hill's, 1601 W. Pine St.
TOURISTS HOMES
Mrs. B. Dedman, W. Caddo St.
Mrs. L. Cooper, W. Pine St.
RESTAURANTS
Hill's, River St.
BARBER SHOPS
Scott's, 6th & Clay St.
Richie's Upright, 16th St.

BRINKLEY
TOURISTS HOMES
Davis, 709 S. Main St.

CAMDEN
HOTELS
Summer Hotel
754½ Adams St. S.W.
TOURIST HOMES
Mrs. Benj. Williams, N. Main St.
Mrs. Hugh Hill, S. Main St.
RESTAURANTS
Jim Summers, 719 S. Main St.
TAVERNS
Daniel's, North Adams St.
Jones, 369 Monroe St.
TAXI CABS
Bradford, Phone 6-9396
LIQUOR STORES
Summers, 715½ S. Main St.

8

SOUTH CAMDEN

ROAD HOUSES
Henry Hanson, 415 Progress S. E.

EL DORADO

HOTELS
Green's, 303 Hill St.
TOURISTS HOMES
C. W. Moore, 5th & Lincoln Ave.
Dr. Dunning, 7th & Columbia Ave.
SERVICE STATIONS
Davidson's

FAYETTEVILLE

.**TOURIST HOMES**
Mrs. S. Mannel, 313 Olive St.
N. Smith, 259 E. Center St.

FORT SMITH

HOTELS
Ullery Inn, 719 N. 9th St.
TOURISTS HOMES
Mrs. Clara E. Oliver
906 North 9th St.
Mrs. Clara E. Oliver, 906 N. 9th St.

HOPE

HOTELS
Lewis-Wilson, 217 E. 3rd St.
RESTAURANTS
Green Leaf, Old 67 Hiway
BEAUTY PARLORS
Unique, 501 S. Hazel St.
BARBER SHOPS
Yeager's, 401 S. Hazel St.
SERVICE STATIONS
Tarßy's Esso, 104 E. 3rd St.
GARAGES
Nun-McDowell, 3rd and Walnut St.
ROAD HOUSES
Fred's, 4th and Hazel Sts.

HOT SPRINGS

HOTELS
Crittenden, 314 Cottage St.
TOURISTS HOMES
New Edmondson, 243 Ash St.
Barabin Villa, 717 Pleasant St.
J. W. Rife, 347½ Malvern Ave.
Mrs. N. Fletcher, 416 Pleasant Ave.
Mrs. C. C. Wilson, 232 Garden St.
BEAUTY SCHOOLS
Hollywood, 310 Church St.
SANITARIUMS
Pythian Baths, 415½ Malvern Ave.

LITTLE ROCK

HOTELS
The Marquette, 522 W. 9th St.
Graysonia, 809 Gaines St.
New Vincent, 522½ West 9th St.
Tucker's, 701½ W. 9th St.
Honeycut, 816 West 9th St.
Charmaine, 820 W. 14th St.

TOURIST HOMES
Mrs. T. Thomas, 1901 High St.
RESTAURANTS
Lafayette, 964 State St.
College, 16th & Bishop
Johnson's, 610 W. 9th St.
DeLuxe, 724 W. 9th St.
Tucker's, 919 Victory St.
C & C, 522½ W. 9th St.
Rainbow, 626 W. 9th St.
Ed's, 1015 Gaines St.
BEAUTY PARLORS
Velvatex, 1004 State St.
Velvia, 814 Chester Ave.
Woods, 1523 High St.
Woods, 16th & High St.
Sue's, 919 W. 5th St.
Fontaine's, 714 West 9th St.
NIGHT CLUBS
Lafayette, 9th & State St.
BARBER SHOPS
Century, 608 W. 9th St.
Elite, 622 W. 9th St.
Fontaine's, 710 West 9th St.
Century, 610 West 9th St.
Woods, 1523 High St.
Friendly, 911 Victory St.
TAVERNS
Majestic, 708 W. 9th St.
LIQUOR STORES
Ritz, 1511 Wright Ave.
Jones, 528 W. 9th St.
Victory, 528 West 9th St.
GARAGES
Lee's, 1401 High St.
TAILORS
Metropolitan, 618 West 9th St.
Crenshaw, 709 W. 9th St.
Ideal, 1005 Apperson St.
SERVICE STATIONS
Lee's, 1401 High St.
Anderson, 8th & State St.
Wrecker, 9th & Gaines St.
GARAGES
Fosters, 1400 W. 10th St.
DRUG STORES
Floyd, 602 W. 9th St.
Children's, 700 W. 9th St.

NORTH LITTLE ROCK

HOTELS
Oasis, 1311 E. 3rd St.
TOURIST HOMES
De Lux Court, 2720 E. Broadway
RESTAURANTS
Jim's, 908 Cedar St. N. L. R.
Nov-Vena, 1101 E. 6th St.
ROAD HOUSES
Oasis, 1311 East 3rd St.

PINE BLUFF

HOTELS
Pee Kay, 300 E. 3rd St.
TOURIST HOMES
M. J. Hollis, 1108 W. 2nd Ave.

9

RESTAURANTS
Shelton's, 200 E. 3rd St.
Duck Inn, 405 N. Cedar St.
BARBER SHOPS
Nappy Chin, 217 State St.
BEAUTY PARLORS
Pruitt's, 1317 W. Baraque St.
BEAUTY SCHOOLS
DeLuxe, 221 E. 3rd St.
Jefferson, 1818 W. 6th Ave.
GARAGES
Alley's, 1101 N. Cedar St.

FORDYSE
RESTAURANTS
Harlem, 211 1st St.

HELENA
SERVICE STATIONS
Stark's, Rightor & Walnut Sts.

RUSSELLVILLE
TOURIST HOMES
E. Latimore, 318 S. Huston Ave.

TEXARKANA
HOTELS
Brown's, 312 W. Elm St.
TOURIST HOMES
G. C. Mackey, 102 E. 9th St.
RESTAURANTS
Grant's Cafe, 830 Laurel St.
BEAUTY PARLORS
M. B. Randell, 1105 Laurel St.

CALIFORNIA
BERKLEY
BEAUTY PARLORS
Little Gem, 1511 Russell St.
BARBER SHOPS
Success, 2946 Sacramento St.

EL CENTRO
RESTAURANTS
Pearl McKinnel Lunch, Box 1049
HOTELS
Roland, 201 E. Main St.

FRESNO
TOURIST HOMES
La Silve, 841 F St.
RESTAURANTS
DeLux, 2193 Ivy St.
New Jerico, 101 Church St.
BEAUTY PARLORS
Rosebud's, 835 G St.
Ruth's, 1816 F St.
Golden West, 1032 F St.
BARBER SHOPS
Golden West, 1032 'F' St.
Magnolia, 602 F St.
Sportsman's, 855 G St.

TAVERNS
26th Century, 1401 F St.
GARAGES
Buddy Lang's, 1658 F St.
Frank's 1326 Fresno St.

HOLLYWOOD
TAILORS
Billy Berg's, 707 N. Ridgewood

IMPERIAL
TOURIST HOMES
Mrs. Albert Bastion, Cor. 7th & M Sts.

LOS ANGELES
HOTELS
Clark Hotel & Annexes
Cor. Washington Blvd. &
Central Ave.
Phone: Prospect 5357
Clark, 1816 So. Central Ave.
La Dale, 862 E. Jefferson Blvd.
Watkins, 2022 N. Adams Blvd. (23)
Lincoln, 549 Ceres Ave.
Norbo, 529 E. 6th St.
Mack's Manor Hotel
1085 W. Jefferson Blvd.
McAlpin, 648 Stanford Ave.
Elite, 1217 Central Ave.
Olympic, 843 S. Central Ave.
Regal, 815 E. 6th St.
Kentucky, 1123 Central Ave.
Dunbar, 4225 S. Central Ave.
TOURIST HOMES
Cashbah Apartments
1189 W. 36th Place
Phone Republic 8290
Vallee Vista, 2408 Cimarron St.
RESTAURANTS
Ivie's, 1105½ E. Vernon Ave.
Henry Bros., 10359 Wilmington
Eddie's, 4201 S. Central Ave.
Zombie, 4216 S. Central Blvd.
Waffle Shop, 1063 E. 43 St.
Clifton's, 618 S. Oliva St.
BEAUTY PARLORS
Sherwoods, 5113 S. Central Ave.
Studio, 2515 S. Central
Continental, 5203 Hopper Ave.
Triangle, 43 San Pedro & Walls Sts
Colonial, 1813½ S. Central Ave.
Dunbar, 4225 S. Central Ave.
Beauty Salon, 1195 East 35th St.
BARBER SHOPS
Bertha's, 1434 W. Jefferson Blvd.
Personality, 4222 S. Central Ave.
Echo, 43rd & Central Ave.

(Los Angeles, continued on 19)

10

The Golden Gate

San Francisco, Calif.

SAN FRANCISCO, the fabulous city by the Golden Gate, offers a mixture of adventure to the tourist.

This great metropolis of the West is said to have become a city overnight. In 1841, just thirty families comprised the entire village now known as San Francisco and in 1850 this same place recorded a population of 25,000 persons of every race, creed and color. Every able-bodied man on receiving news of the precious discovery made by one James W. Marshall on the South Fork of the American River in January of 1848, hurried towards the Golden Gate in pursuit of wealth. Many huge fortunes were amassed during this period. Since that time, San Francisco has never had a dull decade. Its life span has been more exciting than that of many Eastern cities, three times as old. The tourist will observe how the warm shadows of great events and vivid people linger on in this city, keeping it gay and carefree, wise and tolerant. San Franciscans share a common love of and desire to preserve their city's friendly, cosmopolitan way of life.

The strategic location of the city, its magnificent harbor and extensive shipping make it a major port. It possesses one of the finest land-locked harbors in the world. The crescent-shaped street known as the EMBARCADERO, is lined with piers and wharves, which parellels the bay shore

for three and one half miles. Here, amid the seething activity of international trade, the newcomer may stop and pay tribute to the incredible beauty of this harbor whose scenic splendors, it is claimed, rivals Rio de Janiero. Shipping from every quarter of the globe testifies of this city's industrial importance to its country and the world. In the recent Pacific conflict this great port proved its value in another way, by serving as the principal embarkation point for servicemen on their way to uphold the American tradition of honor.

Geography is the element blamed the most, for San Francisco's peculiar weather. The fog and cool summer climate is caused when the heat of the interior valleys sucks the fog and cool air through the Golden Gate. There is no great range of temperature so San Francisco might best be described as enjoying a kind of perpetual autumn. Rain falls mostly in the winter half of the year dividing the seasons into what would normally be winter and summer. September usually heralds San Francisco's bright, sparkling weather which usually lasts until Christmas. However, it is suggested and very strongly too, that a topcoat accompany the newcomer any time of the year because the mornings are cold and the evenings are laughingly described as cool. Despite this strange weather San

GREAT BRIDGE SPANS GOLDEN GATE AT SAN FRANCISCO, CALIFORNIA

At this storied entrance to the continent, where the Pacific Ocean meets San Francisco Bay, stands this monumental red-orange bridge, its towers rising above the strait to the height of a 65-story building . . . the highest, longest-spanned bridge in the world. Its towers are 746 feet high, its center span is 4200 feet long. It has six automobile traffic lanes and two sidewalks.

Francisco is wrapped in atmosphere of enchantment.

San Francisco was once a barren stretch of sand dunes and rocky hills, scattered with swamps and lagoons. In order to provide for its increasing populations its valleys, tidal marshes and lagoons have been filled in and its smaller hills leveled. Today, San Francisco is a city that is largely man-made. The city's famed bridges have united San Francisco with its neighboring municipalities, blending them into one metropolitan area. These bridges consist of two suspensions and one cantilever which when combined, covers over eight miles in length and adds up to the largest bridge structure yet built. The Golden Gate Bridge regarded as the most beautiful bridge structure is also the longest single suspension span in the world. By walking out on it for the price of one dime the tourist can behold this bridge in all its majesty. The San Francisco-Oakland Bay Bridge cannot be seen in this manner though none of its splendor is lost in viewing it from the harbor on a Southern Pacific ferryboat.

Though, the bridges have contributed to their economic and social growth the neighboring communities resent becoming known as San Francisco's bedrooms. Oakland which is California's third largest city is in the same unfavorable position as New York City's, Brooklyn. Industries and assembly plants have turned Oakland into a Western Detroit. Its outstanding symbol of activity is the Latham Square Building, headquarters for Henry Kaiser's vast industrial empire. This city has the largest Negro population on the Pacific Coast.

The University of California is located in Berkeley, the town adjoining Oakland. With more than forty thousand students attending classes on the eight, scattered campuses of the University, Berkeley still manages to be tidy, serene and cordial. It comes closest to achieving the cosmopolitan ease desired by other communities because of its casual acceptance of people regardless of their race, creed or color.

San Francisco however, is fast becoming the focal point of the Negroes' future. Before World War II this city had fewer than 5,000 Negroes. High war wages attracted these people from all over the country to this boom town. More than 45,000 Negroes are squeezed into two areas of San Francisco today, with an estimated thirty-five per cent unemployed. Though, comfortable housing facilities and business opportunities are limited to Negroes at this time, tribute should be paid to the encouraging attitude held by San Franciscans toward the improvement and eventual erasure of these existing conditions. They pride themselves on living in the most cultured, cosmopolitan and liberal com-

SAN FRANCISCO'S CHINATOWN

13

munity in the entire west and as a result are truly, exerting a sincere effort to maintain this position. Many Negroes are of course, proving their value to this community daily and justifying the opportunities presented to them.

In order to pursue their earnest interest in the cultural side of life, San Franciscans dig deep into their private and public funds. Their city is one of the very few where the symphony and opera groups are maintained by the support of every taxpayer. Its symphonic orchestra is one of the foremost in the country while its operatic group is fast gaining recognition. It should be mentioned that art of every kind is appreciated year-round and include fine art shows, lectures, concerts and theatres, for the tourist and art lovers' benefit. San Francisco owns its Opera House which is magnificent and famed as the place where the United Nations' charter was framed. It seems appropriate to San Franciscans that their city, with its people from many lands, was the birthplace of an organization designed to bring world peace.

The Cable Cars, which are a source of amazement and amusement to the newcomer, are a San Francisco institution. The city's hills account for their continued use. In their early days of existence they enabled the town to expand up these steep hills. A beautiful marine view is enjoyed by tens of thousands of San Franciscans from their living room windows atop these hills today, as a result of these comic yet picturesque vehicles. When a more modern method of transportation was proposed by the Transportation Committee, it was overwhelmingly voted against by a group, who represented those San Franciscans who, dismiss any inconveniences suffered enroute from their homes on high to their downtown office and who, rather enjoy the thrill of being crushed inside or hanging helter-skelter from any side of these quaint cars.

San Francisco's downtown area is compact and accesible as clusters of skyscrapers house banks, public buildings and business houses. The shopping district centers on Union Square where department stores, smart women's shops, furriers, fine book stores, hotels, theaters and specialty shops can all be located. It is an area of bustling activity and hurrying throngs, punctuated on every other street corner by the inevitable sidewalk flower stand which offers a colorful assortment of flowers to the busy yet appreciative passer-by. This downtown area is not only the center of San Francisco's economic life but also a point from which every fascinating district in the city can be found.

Like every famous city, San Francisco has its cherished land marks. The Presidio, which was formerly a garrison for Spanish soldiers is steeped in California's early history and heads the list of interesting sights in this city, as does Portsmouth Square, known as San Francisco's birthplace; the Mission District, the very oldest and most densely populated area; the San Francisco Terminal Building and the Donahue Monument. Of course Lotta's Fountain is a MUST on every visitor's list. It was formerly a watering trough for horses presented by the greatest Western belle of them all, Miss Lotta Crabtree, to the city of gold, during the exciting days of old. This gift has been transformed into a drinking fountain for humans and is the pride of every San Franciscan's heart. Yacht Harbor. Seal Rocks and the Fleishhacker Pool

14

THE SAN FRANCISCO-OAKLAND BAY BRIDGE, SAN FRANCISCO, CALIFORNIA

This bridge is the largest in the world, 8¼ miles long; 4½ miles over navigable water. The view is toward San Francisco from Yerba Buena Island in mid-bay, through which rocky island, of 110 acres the bridge passes by a tunnel and then goes on by leaps of mighty spans to Oakland. The west half of the bridge, seen in the picture, consists of two suspension bridges anchored in the center to a concrete pier. The bridge is double-decked, with six lanes for automobiles on its upper deck, and three lanes for trucks and buses and two trucks for electric trains on its lower deck.

15

OCEAN BEACH AT SAN FRANCISCO, CALIFORNIA

San Francisco meets the Pacific Ocean on a long white beach, which extends some three and a half miles between the Cliff House and Fleishhacker Zoo. It is skirted by the Esplanade and the Great Highway; flanked by Playland-at-the-Beach and Golden Gate Park. Here people wade into waves from China; cast in the surf for striped bass and other fish; bask around picnic fires on the sand; point their cars west and watch the sea and ships or a sunset; enjoy entertainment at the playland. Golden Gate Park extends from here four miles to the center of the city.

16

Fishermen's Wharf is one of the sights of San Francisco. Located some three miles within the Golden Gate, it is like a bit of the Bay of Naples set down on the shore of San Francisco Bay. From the piers of the lagoons where some 350 fishing vessels berth, one has an excellent view of the Golden Gate Bridge and of the hills of the north shore piling up to the 2600 feet height of lordly Mount Tamalpais. Behind the wharf is Telegraph Hill with high Coit Tower on top. It is the visual center of the Latin Quarter in the North Beach section of San Francisco.

provide varied interests in water sports, while Golden Gate offers an atmosphere of great natural beauty with its 1,013 acres of flowers, shrubs, trees and lawns along with its recreational activities, refreshment enclosures and educational facilities.

Fisherman's Wharf is located at the end of the Embarcadero and is one of the most picturesque areas in San Francisco. Crews, of the gaily painted fishing fleet, tend their business, completely oblivious of the tourists' interest. A spirit of good fellowship prevails among these men as they share their boats, their gear and their profits. Their naturalness is an education and delight to the stranger. Along the street are stands displaying shellfish and at the curb, big, iron cauldrons boil large freshly caught crabs for the purchaser's immediate or delayed consumption. Neighboring restaurants

have captured this Old World atmosphere and presents it, and recently caught dinners in a more fashionable manner to their patrons.

The Latin Quarter is one of the biggest tourist attractions in this city because it is a section of many nationalities. French, Negro, Spanish, Portugese and Italians are all found here. These people are devoted to the entertainment requirements of its many visitors. Everyone turns to its interesting district for a variety of foods and cabarets. From bawdy examples of San Francisco's hospitality, one may turn to more elegance and sophistication within a few short steps in this fascinating part of the city.

San Francisco's Chinatown is the largest Chinese settlement outside the Orient. It is an orderly section today. The old Chinatown of brothels, gambling houses, opium dens and slums was destroyed in the great fire of 1906. Today exotic, pagoda roof tops and iron grilled balconies appear side by side with American tin roofs and straight fronts while men and women of Old China, mingle harmoniously with those who have adopted the latest occidental fashions. In exploring this part of San Francisco, the visitor's interest is captivated by the Chinese Telephone Exchange. This is a triple-pagoda building of traditional Chinese architecture completed with red and gold trimmed, lacquer dragons. Here, attractive Chinese girls operate the switchboards and are acquainted with every subscriber's street and telephone number. Naturally these girls have created a precedent in telephone operating efficiency. Chinatown on the whole is a section which offers fine silks, carved ivory, lacquer-ware and trinkets of every kind to the newcomer along with famous eating places and night clubs. The Chinese

New Year celebration brings forth, with increased vigor, this section's best qualities. The streets are gaily lined with flower stands and every shrine in every shop is lavishly decorated while a spirit of genuine good will and revelry prevails.

The tourist will find San Francisco adaptable, elastic and truly cosmopolitan through the blending of the talents provided by its people. The Italians' love of operatic music, the Mexicans' joy of festivals, the French flair for style and the Spaniards' interest in romance are tempered by the wisdom of the Chinese, the vigor of Midwestern and Eastern settlers and most recently, the beloved humor and wit of the Negro. They have all contributed to San Francisco's mixed flavor and provide it with a viewpoint unlimited by horizons. Your trip to this Western city will be a thrilling experience indeed.

(First cover photo)

CABLE CARS CLIMB STEEP HILLS IN SAN FRANCISCO, CALIFORNIA

Cable cars were invented in San Francisco, in 1873, to climb that city's hills. People find them charming and festive there today in their roller-coaster, bell-Street cable line climbs from Market Street to the top of Nob Hill, passing ringing journeys. Here the California through the financial district and Chinatown on the way. On the height, where once stood the palaces of railroad and bonanza millionaires, are hotels and apartment houses. From the Top of the Mark there one enjoys superlative views of the city, bay and surrounding hills.

(Fourth cover photo)

MISSION SAN FRANCISCO DE ASIS, SAN FRANCISCO, CALIFORNIA

With the founding of Mission San Francisco de Asis, on June 29, 1776, San Francisco was begun—five days before the Liberty Bell in Philadelphia rang forth its historic tidings Situated near the center of the city, it is popularly known as Mission Dolores. Within its adobe walls, which are four feet thick, one sees ancient altars from Mexico and original decorative work of Indian neophytes on ceiling and walls. The "new church" next the old mission, is an example of Spanish architecture. On the other side of the mission is its ancient cemetery, with its "Grotto of Lourdes" and headstones recalling many notables and others of San Francisco's early days.

18

(Los Angeles, cont. from p. 10)

(Los Angeles, cont. from p. 10)

TAVERNS
Margot, 5259 S. Central Ave.
Golden Gate, 1719 E. 103rd St.
Paradise, 5505 S. Central Ave.
Samba, 5th & Towns Ave.
Tip Top Cafe, 4631 S. Central Ave.
Johnson's, 4201 S. Main St.
Elks Lounge, 10123 Beach

NIGHT CLUBS
Basket Room, 3219 S. Central Ave.
Harlem, 11812 Parmalee
Wakeki, 8741 So. Western Ave.
Last Word, 4206 So. Central Ave.

LIQUOR STORES
Dunbar, 4223 S. Central Ave.
Jackson's, 5501 S. Central Ave.
Esquire, Vernon & Central Ave.
W. M. Davis, 4821 Long Beach Ave.
Fred Little John, 3593 Avalon Blvd.

SERVICE STATIONS
Valentine's Service, 2657 S. Western Ave.
Carner's, 4500 S. Avalon Ave.
Simpkins & Cower, 2227 S. Central Ave.
Tom's, 1424 W. Jefferson Blvd.
Hughes, 2901 W. Jefferson Blvd.
Brock, 1246 W. Jefferson Blvd.
Garcia, 52nd Pl. & Central
Wilkens, 4924 S. Central Ave.
Gracis, 5201 S. Central Ave.
Watson Bros., 4000 So. Pedro St.

GARAGES
Parkers, 10229 Alameda
Alexander's, Jefferson & Griffith

DRUG STORES
Allums, 4375 S. Central Ave.
Doctor's, 4012 S. Central Ave.
Medical, 3112 S. Western Ave.

TAILORS
Bader's, 1840 E. 103rd St.
Delta, 8512 Compton Ave.
Benjamin, 5016 So. Central Ave.

REAL ESTATE
Herndon, 3419 So. Central Ave.

LAKE ELSIMORE

HOTELS
Geo. Moore, 407 Scrivener St.
Lake Elsimore, 416 N. Kelogg St.

OAKLAND

HOTELS
Paradise, 1793 7th St.
Ebony Plaza, 3908 San Pablo Ave.
Carver, 1412 Market St.
Warren, 1252 7th St.

TOURIST HOMES
Mrs. A. C. Clark, 805 Linden St.
Mrs. H. Williams, 3521 Grove St.

RESTAURANTS
The Villa, 3016 Adeline St.

TAVERNS
Overland Cafe, 1719 7th St.

SERVICE STATIONS
McCabe, 5901 Adeline St.
Signal, 800 Center St.

GARAGES
Bufford's, 5901 Aldine St.

PERRIS

TOURIST HOMES
Muse-A-While

PASADENA

SERVICE STATIONS
Penn Mobile, 1096 Lincoln Ave.

SACRAMENTO

HOTELS
Center Hotel, 420½ Capitol Ave.

TOURIST HOMES
Mrs. R. C. Peyton 2202½ 4th St.

RESTAURANTS
Dunlap's, 4372 4th Ave.

BARBER SHOPS
Mrs. Mikes, 1350 56th St.

BEAUTY PARLORS
Twigg's, 421 Capitol Ave.
Leftridge, 3162 Sacramento Blvd.
Nannette's, 1214 5th St.
Larocco's, 1630 7th St.

NIGHT CLUBS
Mo-Mo, 600 Capitol Ave.

DRUG STORES
Taylors, 1250 6th St.

SAN DIEGO

HOTELS
Douglas, 206 Market St.
Simmons, 542 6th Ave.
Y.W.C.A., 1029 C St.

RESTAURANTS
Sun, 421 Market St.
Brown Hostess, 2816 Imperial Ave.

SERVICE STATIONS
Webber's, 1655 1st Ave.
Woodson's, 3126 Franklin Ave.

LIQUOR STORES
Robinson's, 2876 Imperial Ave.

TAILORS
Clever, 2606 Imperial Ave.
Imperial, 2751 Imperial Ave.
Ramona, 2244 Logan Ave.
Maryann, 1317 Market St.

SAN FRANCISCO

HOTELS
The Scaggs, 1715 Webster St.
New Pullman, 232 Townsend St.
Edison, 1540 Ellis St.
Texas, 1840 Filmore St.
Buford, 1969 Sutter St.

TOURIST HOMES
Mrs. F. Johnson, 1758 Sutter St.
Thadd's DeLux, 2040 Sutter St.

19

RESTAURANTS
Hi-Lo, 1686 O'Farrell St.
BARBER SHOPS
Hillside, 5267 3rd St.
TAVERNS
Jack's, 1931 Sutter St.
NIGHT CLUBS
Town Club, 1963 Sutter St.
The Plantation, 1628 Post St.
Flamingo, 1836 Filmore St.
DRUG STORES
Riggan's, 2600 Sutter St.
Olympic, Cor. Jones & Post
Jim's, 1698 Sutter St.
LIQUOR STORES
Sullivan, 1623 Post St.
Coast, 1567 Tillmore St.

TULARE
TOURIST HOMES
South "K" St., 330 South "K" St.
TAVERNS
King's, 322-24 South K St.

VALLEJO
TAVERNS
Cotton Club, Virginia & Branciforte

VICTORVILLE
TOURIST HOMES
Murray's Dude Ranch
Raglan Guest Ranch, Box 457

COLORADO

BOULDER
RESTAURANTS
Ray's Inn, 2038 Goss St.

COLORADO SPRINGS
TOURIST HOMES
G. Roberts, 418 E. Cucharras St.

DENVER
HOTELS
Bean Hotel, 2152 Arapahoe St.
TOURIST HOMES
Mrs. G. Anderson, 2119 Marion St,
**Mrs. George L. Anderson
2119 Marion St.
Mrs. Ila G. Burton, 3430 Race St.
Mrs. Harney E. Blair,
2936 Gaylord St.**
Mrs. Hattie Graves, 3052 Humboldt St.
RESTAURANTS
Green Lantern, 2859 Fremont
Da-Nite, 1430 22nd Ave.
Atlas, 611 27th St.
B & E, 2847 Gilpin St.
BEAUTY PARLORS
Landers, 2460 Marion St.
Ford, 2527 Humboldt St.

BARBER SHOPS
Roxy, 2559 Welton St.
26th Century, 2727 Welton St.
TAVERNS
Rossonian Lounge, 2650 Welton St.
Arcade, 739 E. 26th Ave.
Archie's, 2449 Larimer St.
LIQUOR STORES
Lincoln, 2636 Welton St.
Aristocrat, 3101 William St.
18th Ave., 1314 E. 17th Ave.
SERVICE STATIONS
Da-Nite, 729 E. 26th Ave.
White, 2555 Downing St.
Plazer, E. 22nd & Humboldt Sts.
TAXI CABS
Ritz, 2721 Welton St.
DRUG STORES
T. K., 27th & Larimer Sts.
Ideal, 28th & Downing
V. H. Meyers, 22nd & Downing Sts
Radio, Welton at 26th St.
TAILORS
Arcade 729 E. 26th St.
White House, 2863 Welton St.
Ace, 2290 Downing St.

DUMONT
LODGES
Mountain Studio

GREELEY
TOURIST HOMES
Mrs. E. Alexander, 106 E. 12th St.

LA JUNTA
TOURIST HOMES
Mrs. Moore, 301 Lewis Ave.

LA MAR
HOTELS
Alamo
RESTAURANTS
Joe's

MONTROSE
HOTELS
Adams
RESTAURANTS
Chipeta Cafe
BEAUTY SHOPS
Ace
SERVICE STATIONS
Sorenson Sinclair Station
GARAGES
Gilbert Motor Co.

PUEBLO
TOURIST HOMES
Mrs. T. Protho, 918 E. Evans Ave.
TAVERNS
Blue Bird, 705 N. Main St.
Mecca Grill, 719 N. Main St.
Grand, 114 W. 4th St.

20

CONNECTICUT

BRIDGEPORT

HOTELS
Y.W.C.A., Golden Hill St.
TOURIST HOMES
Mrs. M. Barrett , 83 Summer St.

HARTFORD

TOURIST HOMES
Mrs. Johnson, 2016 Main St.
BEAUTY SHOPS
Quality, 1762 Main St.
BARBER SHOPS
Williams, 1975 Main St.
DRUG STORES
Bellevue, 256 Bellevue St.
LIQUOR STORES
Harry's, 2574 Main St.
Canton, 1736 Main St.
Ben's, 1988 Main St.
The Paramount, 107 Canton St.
Bacon, 81 Homestead Ave.
TAVERNS
Bancroft's. Main & Elmer Sts.
Club Sundown, 360 Windsor St.
Franks Tavern, 257 Windsor St.
SERVICE STATIONS
Ware's, 34 Spring St.
Cauls, 2750 Main St.

NEW HAVEN

HOTELS
Portsmouth, 91 Webster St.
TOURIST HOMES
Dr. M. F. Allen, 65 Dixwell Ave.
RESTAURANTS
Monterey, 267 Dixwell Ave.
Belmonts, 156 Dixwell Ave.
BEAUTY PARLORS
Mme. Ruby, 175 Goffe St.
Gialy's, 624 Orchard St.
Ethel's, 152 Dixwell Ave.
Harris, 734 Orchard St.
SCHOOL OF BEAUTY CULTURE
Modern, 170 Goffe St.
NIGHT CLUBS
Elk's, 204 Goffe St.
Lillian's Paradise, 137 Wallace St.
LIQUOR STORES
Shiffrins, 221 Dixwell Ave.
DRUG STORES
Proctor's, 180 Dixwell Ave.

NEW LONDON

TOURIST HOMES
Mrs. E. Whittle, 735 Bank St.

SOUTH NORWALK

HOTELS
Palm Gardens, Post Rd.

STAMFORD

HOTELS
GLADSTONE. Gay St.
TOURIST HOMES
Robert Graham, 27 Hanrahan Ave.
NIGHT CLUBS
Sizone, 136 W. Main St.

WATERBURY

HOTELS
Elton
TOURIST HOMES
Community House, 34 Hopkins St.
DRUG STORES
Rhineharts, 471 N. Main St.
McCarthy, Main, Bishop & Grove
Sts.
TAILOR SHOPS
Sam's, 149 South Main St.

WEST HAVEN

HOTELS
Dadds, 359 Beach St.
Seaview, 392 Beach St.
TAVERNS
Hoot Owl, 374 Beach St.

DELAWARE

DOVER

HOTELS
Cannon's, Kirkwood St.
Dean's, Forrest St.
Mosely's, Division St.

LAUREL

RESTAURANTS
Joe Randolph's, W. 6th St.
BARBER SHOPS
Joe Randolph's, W. 6th St.
BEAUTY PARLORS
Orchid, W. 6th St.

TOWNSEND

HOTELS
Rodney, Dupont Highway-Rt. 13
GARAGES
Hood's, Dupont Hiway

WILMINGTON

HOTELS
Royal, 703 French St.
Lawson, 203 Poplar St.
Y.M.C.A., 10th & Walnut Sts.
Y.W.C.A., 10th & Walnut Sts.
TOURIST HOMES
Miss W. A. Brown, 1306 Tatnall St
Mrs. E. Till, 1008 French St.
RESTAURANTS
Christian Assn. Bldg., 10th &
Walnut Sts.

21

BEAUTY SHOPS
Mrs. M. Anderson, 916 French St.
Dora's, 314 East 10th St.
NIGHT CLUBS
Spot, 7th & 8th on French St.
SERVICE STATIONS
Esso, 8th & 9th on King

DISTRICT OF COLUMBIA

WASHINGTON, D. C.

HOTELS
Johnson's Hotel, 1505 13th St. N. W.
Whitelaw, 13th & "T" Sts. N. W.
Johnson, Jr., 1509 Vermont Ave., N. W.
Dunbar, U St. & 15th St., N. W.
Y.M.C.A., 1816 12th St., N. W.
Y.W.C.A., 901 Rhode Is. Ave., N. W.
Logan, 13th & Logan Circle N. W.
Clore, 614 'S' St. N. W.
Cadillac, 1500 Vermont St. N. W.
Ken Rod, 621 Rhode Island Ave., N. W.
Charles, 1334 'R' St. N. W.
TOURIST HOMES
Jannie's, 939 Rhode Is. Ave. N. W.
Buddie's, 1320 5th St. N. W.
Towles, 1321 13th St. N. W.
Towles, 1342 Vermont Ave., N. W.
Modern, 3006 13th St., N. W.
Rivers, 1021 Monroe St., N. W.
Patsy's, 2026 13th St., N. W.
Cottage Grove, 1531 Vermont Ave., N. W.
Terry's, 939 Rhode Is. Ave., N. W.
Boyd's, 1744 Swann St., N. W.
Edward's, 1837 16th St., N. W.
TAVERNS
Grand Casa Blanca, 3413 Georgia Ave. N. W.
New Hollywood, 1940 9th St. N. W.
Holleywood, 1940 9th St., N. W.
Harrison's Cafe, 455 Florida Ave., N. W.
Off Beat, 1849 7th St., N. W.
Kenyon, Ga. Ave. & Kenyon St., N. W.
Herbert's Stage Door, 618 "T" St., N. W.
RESTAURANTS
Republic Gardens, 1355 'U' St. N. W.
Alfreds, 1610 'U' St. N. W.
Keys, 7th & "T" St., N. W.
Chicken Paradise, 1210 U. St., N. W.
Earl's, 1218 U. St., N. W.

Sugar Bowl, 2830 Georgia Ave., N. W.
Shrimp Hut, 807 Florida Ave., N. W.
Uptown, 807 Florida, N. W.
Johnson's, 1909 14th St., N. W.
The Hour, 1937 11th St., N. W.
Cozy, 708 Florida Ave., N. W.
Kenyon Grill, 3119 Georgia Ave., N. W.
The Hour, 1837 11th St., N. W.
LIQUOR STORES
Peoples, 719 11th St., N. W.
S & W, 1428 9th St., N. W.
Shuster's, 101 H St., N. W.
Ney's, 1013 Penna. Ave., N. W.
Carter's, 1927 14th St., N. W.
BARBER SHOPS
Florida, 1803 Florida Ave., N. W.
Blue Bird, 3219 Georgia Ave. N. W.
Harpers, 703 Park Rd.
York, 3634 Georgia Ave. N. W.
BEAUTY PARLORS
Modes, 3100 Georgia Ave. N. W.
Al, Lenes 3551 Georgia Ave. N. W.
Henretta's, 3616 Georgia Ave. N. W.
Apex, 1417 'U' St., N. W.
The Royal, 1860 'T' St., N. W.
Elite, 1806 Florida Ave., N. W.
Lil's, 1416 9th St., N. W.
Green's, 1825 18th St., N. W.
Bandbox, 2036 18th St., N. W.
La Salle, 541 Florida Ave., N. W.
NIGHT CLUBS
Republic Gardens, 1355 U St., N. W.
Club Bali, 1901 14th St., N. W.
Club Caverns, 11th & U St., N. W.
Ebony, Cor. 7th & 'S' Sts. N. W.
SERVICE STATIONS
Brown's, 3128 Ga. Ave., N. W.
Engelberg, 1783 Florida Ave., N. W.
TAILORS
W. R. Reynolds, 1808 Florida Ave., N. W.

FLORIDA

DAYTONA BEACH
LIQUOR STORES
Hank's, 531 S. Campbell St.

DELRAY BEACH
TAVERNS
Manfield, N. W. 1st St.

FORT LAUDERDALE
HOTELS
Hill, 430 N. W. 7th Ave.

22

JACKSONVILLE

HOTELS
Richmond, 422 Broad St.
Blue Chip, 514 Broad St.
TOURIST HOMES
Craddock, 45th & Moncrief
E. H. Flipper, 739 W. Church St.
L. D. Jefferson, 1838 Moncrief Rd.
B. Robinson, 128 Orange St.
C. H. Simmons, 134 W. Ashley St.
NIGHT CLUBS
Two Spots, 45th & Moncrief Rd.
Manuel's, 624-629 W. Ashley St.
BARBER SHOPS
Blue Chip, 516 Broad St.
RESTAURANTS
Sunrise, 829 Pearl St.
Blu-Goose, 1303 Davis St.
DRUG STORES
Imperial, Broad & Ashley Sts.
Smith's, 613 Ashley St.

LAKE CITY

TOURIST HOMES
Mrs. M. McCoy, 730 E. Leon St.
Rivers, 931 Taylor St.
Mrs. B. J. Jones, 720 E. Leon St.
RESTAURANTS
Bill Rivers, 931 Taylor St.
BARBER SHOPS
George's, 302 E. Railroad St.
SERVICE STATIONS
Farmenis, 300 E. Washington St.
GARAGES
Chicken's, E. Railroad St.

LAKELAND

TOURIST HOMES
Mrs. J. Davis, 842½ N. Fla. Ave.
Mrs. A. Davis, 518 W., 1st St.

LAKE WALES

RESTAURANTS
Hills Dew Drop Inn
47 "B" St.

MIAMI

HOTELS
Mary Elizabeth, 642 N. W. 2nd Ave.
Dorsey, 941 N. W. 2nd Ave.
Lord Calvert, 216 N. W. 6th St.
BEAUTY PARLORS
..lizabeth, 175 N. W. 11th Terrace
BEAUTY SCHOOLS
Sunlight, 1011 N. W. 2nd Ave.
TAVERNS
Star, 3rd Ave. & 15th St., N. W.

LIQUOR STORES
Cuban, 1701 N. W. 4th Ave.
Ideal, 175 N. W. 11th St.
Henry's, 379 N. W. 14th St.
TAILORS
Valet, 596 N. W. 14th St.

ORLANDO

HOTELS
Wells Bilt, 509 W. South St.

PENSACOLA

HOTELS
Grand, 2618 N. Guillemarde St.
RESTAURANTS
Rhumboogie, 509 E. Salamanca St.
TAILORS
Reese, 307 E. Wright St.
New-Way, 1021 N. 9th Ave.
DRUG STORES
Hannah, 198 N. Palafax
LIQUOR STORES
Two Spot, 316 N. Devillier St.
RESTAURANTS
Brown's, 406 Lemon St.

SOUTH JACKSONVILLE

RESTAURANTS
Cool Spot, 2619 Kings Ave.

ST. PETERSBURG

Mrs. M. C. Henderson, 2580 9th St.

ST. AUGUSTINE

TOURIST HOMES
F. H. Kelly, 83 Bridge St.

TAMPA

HOTELS
Afro, 722 La Salle St.
Rogers, 1025 Central Ave.
Pyramid, 1023 Central Ave.
Dallas, 829 Zack St.
TAVERNS
Little Savoy, Central & Scott
Peach, 1002 6th Ave.
Manuel's Place, 1608 N. Blvd.
Brittwood, 1320 Main St.
Paradise, 201 Robert St.
Atomic, 3813 29th St.
TAILORS
Elizabeth, 175 N. W. 11th Terrace
Alvarez, 931 E. Broadway
DRUG STORES
Wells, "K" & Nebraska Ave.
LIQUOR STORES
Reo-Franklin, Cor. Lafayette
Tampa St. Liquor Store
GARAGES
Calvins, 1408 Orange St.

23

GEORGIA

ADRIAN
TOURIST HOME
Wayside, U. S. Rt. 80

ALBANY
TOURIST HOMES
Mrs. A. J. Ross, 514 Mercer St.
Mrs. L. Davis, 313 South St.
Mrs. C. Washington, 228 S. Jackson
St.

ATLANTA
HOTELS
Hotel Royal. 214 Auburn Ave., N. E.
Mack, 548 Bedford Place. N. E.
Shaw, 245 Auburn Ave., N. E.
Y.M.C.A., 22 Butler St.
Waluhaje, 239 W. Lake Ave., N. W.
Savoy, 239 Auburne Ave., N. E.
TOURIST HOME
Connally, 125 Walnut St., S. W.
RESTAURANTS
Suttons, 312 Auburn Ave., N. E.
Joe's Coffee Bar, 200 Auburn Ave.
Paschal Bros., 837 Hunter St. N. W.
TAVERNS
The Blackaret, 848 Mayson Turner
Ave.
Yeah Man, 256 Auburn Ave., N. E.
Sportmans Smoke Shop, 242 Auburn
Ave., N. E.
Butler's, 1868 Simpson Rd.
BEAUTY PARLORS
Poro, 250½ Auburn Ave.
Camolene, 859½ Hunter St.
BARBER SHOPS
R. W. Woodard, 160 Elm St., S. W.
Artistic, 55 Decatur
Gate City, 240 Auburn Ave., N. W.
Silver Moon, 202 Auburn Ave.
NIGHT CLUBS
Posnciana, 143 Auburn Ave.
SERVICE STATIONS
Hall's, 215 Auburn Ave., N. E.
GARAGES
South Side, 539 Fraser St., N. E.
TAILORS
Spic & Span, 907 Hunter St., N. W.

AUGUSTA
HOTELS
Crimm's, 725 9th St.
LQIUOR STORES
Bollinger's, 1114 Gwennett St.

BRUNSWICK
TOURIST HOMES
The Palms, 1309 Glouster St.
Melody Tourist Inn, 1505 G. St.
RESTAURANTS
Green Lantern, 1615 Albany St.
BARBER SHOPS
Battle's, 1304 Gloucester St.

BEAUTY PARLORS
Ethel's, 1501 London St.
GARAGE
Gould's, 1603 New Castle St.
TAXI CABS
Murphy's, 201 "F" St.
TAVERNS
Duncan, 1100 Gloucester St.

COLUMBUS
HOTELS
Lowe's, 724 5th Ave.
Y.M.C.A., 521 9th Ave.
RESTAURANTS
BEAUTY PARLORS
BARBER SHOPS
Sherrell's, 1st Ave.
NIGHT CLUBS
Golden Rest, 1026 7th Ave.
GARAGES
Seventh Avenue, 816 7th Ave.

DOUGLAS
HOTELS
Economy, Cherry St.
TOURIST HOMES
Lawson's, Pearl St.
RESTAURANTS
Thomas', Pearl St.
BARBER SHOPS
Tucker & Mathis, Cherry St.
BEAUTY PARLORS
Rosella's, Gaskin St.
SERVICE STATIONS
Lonnie A. Pope, Peterson St.
TAVERNS
Sport Harold's, Coffee St.
ROAD HOUSES
Violet Tyson, Cherry St.

DUBLIN
TOURIST HOMES
Mrs. R. Hunter, 504 S. Jefferson

EASTMAN
TOURIST HOMES
J. P. Cooper, 211 College St.

MACON
HOTELS
Richmond, 335 Broadway
RESTAURANTS
Jean's, 545 Cotton Ave.
BEAUTY PARLORS
Lula Life, 283 2nd St.
TAILORS
Herschel, 284 Broadway
SERVICE STATIONS
Anderson's, Pursley at Pond St.

SAVANNAH
TOURIST HOMES
Elizabethian, 512 W. Park Ave.
BEAUTY PARLORS
Rose, 348 Price St.

SERVICE STATIONS
Gibson's, 442 West Broad St.
DRUG STORES
Moore's, 37th & Florence

STATESBORO
TOURIST HOMES
Debbie's, 210 Roundtree Ext.

THOMASVILLE
HOTELS
Imperial, Tallahassee Highway

WAY CROSS
HOTELS
TOURIST HOMES
Mrs. K. G. Scarlett, 843 Reynolds
RESTAURANTS
Paradise, Oak St.
BARBER SHOPS
Johnson's, Oak St.
SERVICE STATIONS
Union Cab, State St.

ILLINOIS

CHICAGO
HOTELS
Manor House, 4635 So. Parkway
Ritz Hotel, 409 East Oakwood Blvd.
Hotel Como, 5204-6 South Parkway
Du Sable, 764 Oakwood Blvd.
Evans Hotel, 733 East 61st St.
Pershing Hotel, 6400 Cottage Grove Ave.
Southway Hotel, 6014 S. Parkway
Spencer Hotel, 300 E. Garfield Blvd.
Grand Hotel, 5044 South Parkway
Y.M.C.A., 3763 South Parkway
S & S, 4142 South Parkway
Y.W.C.A., 4559 South Parkway
Monarch Hotel, 4530 Prairie Ave.
Albion Hotel, 4009 Lake Park Ave.
Prairie Hotel, 2836 Prairie Ave.
Eberhart Hotel, 6050 Eberhart Ave.
The Don Hotel, 3337 Michigan Ave.
Harlem Hotel, 5020 S. Michigan Ave.
South Central, 520 E. 47th St.
Loretta, 6201 Vernon Ave.
Garfield, 231 E. Garfield Blvd.
Vienna, 3921 Indiana Ave.
Wedgewood Towers, 64th & Woodlawn
Sutherland, 47th & Drexel Blvd.
Strand, Cottage Grove & 63 St.
TOURIST HOMES
Day's, 3616 South Parkway
Poro College, 4415 S. Parkway

RESTAURANTS
Morris' 410 E. 47th St.
Wrights, 3753 S .Wabash Ave.
A. & J. 105 E. 51st St.
Pitts, 812 E. 39th St.
Pioneer, 533 E. 43rd St.
Parkway, 429 East 45th St.
BEAUTY PARLORS
Matties', 4212 Cottage Grove Ave.
BARBER SHOPS
Bank's, 209 E. 39th St.
TAVERNS
The Palm, 466 E. 47th St.
El Casino, 823 E. 39th St.
Key Hole, 3965 S. Parkway
NIGHT CLUBS
Show Boat, 6109 Parkway
820 Club, 820 E. 39th St.
Delux, 6323 So. Parkway
SERVICE STATIONS
Parkway, 340 W. Grand Ave.
Standard, Garfield & S. Parkway
GARAGES
Zephyr, 4535 S. Cottage Grove Ave.
AUTOMOTIVE
Charles Baron, 3840 Michigan Ave.
DRUG STORES
Thompson, 545 E. 47th St.
TAILORS
Perkin, 4109 So. State St.
LIQUOR STORES
Sam's, 2255 W. Madison St.

DANVILLE
HOTELS
Stewarts, East North St.
Just A Mere Hotel, 218 E. North St.
TOURIST HOMES
Mrs. Lillian Wheeler, 109 Hayes St.

CENTRALIA
TOURIST HOMES
Mrs. Claybourne, 303 N. Pine St.
BEAUTY SHOPS
M. Coleman, 503 N. Poplar St.
BARBER SHOPS
P. Coleman, 503 N. Poplar St.
SERVICE STATIONS
Langenfield, 120 N. Poplar St.

EAST ST. LOUIS
TOURIST HOMES
P. B. Reeves, 1803 Bond Ave.
W. E. Officer, 2114 Missouri Ave.

PEORIA
TOURIST HOMES
Clara Gibons, 923 Monson St.
BARBER SHOPS
Stone's, 323 N. Adams St.
NIGHT CLUBS
Bris Collins, 405 N. Washington St.

SPARTA
HOTELS
Midtown Hotel & Country Club

25

SPRINGFIELD
TOURIST HOMES
Dudley Tourist Rest
130 So. 11th St.
Madell Dudley, 1211 E. Adams
Mrs. L. Jones, 1230 E. Jefferson
Mrs. M. Rollins, 844 S. College St.
Mrs. B. Mosby, 1614 E. Jackson St.
Mrs. G. Bell, 625 N. 2nd St.
Mrs. E. Brooks, 705 N. 2nd St.
Dr. Ware, 1520 E. Washington St.
Mrs. Lula Stuart, 1615 E. Jefferson St.
Mrs. Bernie Eskridge, 1501 E. Jackson St.
BEAUTY PARLORS
Mrs. Mildred Ousley, 1228 So. 14th St.
Cozy Corner, 1229 E. Adams St.
BARBER SHOPS
Streamline, 835 E. Washington St.
Clem & Sikes, 120 So. 11th St.
TAVEVRNS
Cansler, 807 E. Washington St.
George White, 817 E. Washington St.
Panama, 120 So. 11th St.
Rose Lee, 1015 So. 17th St.
SERVICE STATIONS
Leon Stewart, 1400 E. Jefferson St.
DRUG STORES
Ideal Drug Store, 801 E. Washington St.

ROCKFORD
HOTELS
Briggs, 429 S. Court St.
TOURIST HOMES
Mrs. C. Gorum, 301 Steward Ave.
S. Westbrook, 630 Lexington Ave.
Mrs. Brown, 927 S. Winnebago St.

IDAHO
BOISE
TOURIST HOMES
Mrs. S. Love, 1164 River St.
Open Door Mission, 1159 River St.
RESTAURANTS
Union Pacific Greyhound Depot, 9th & Bannock St.

POCATELLO
TOURIST HOMES
A.M.E. Parsnge, 625 E. Fremont
Tourist Park, E. Fremont St.

INDIANA
ELKHART
TOURIST HOMES
Miss E. Botts, 336 St. Joe St.

EVANSVILLE
TOURIST HOMES
Mrs. Lauderdale, 608 Cherry St.
Miss F. Snow, 719 Oak St.
Community Ass'n, 626 Cherry St.

FORT WAYNE
HOTELS
Hotel Howell
1803 S. Hanna St.
Phone: H 5304
TOURIST HOMES
Mrs. B. Talbot, 456 E. Douglas
RESTAURANTS
Leo Manuals', 1329 Lafayette St.
Stewart's, 621 E. Brackenridge St.
Martin & Rankin, 1329 S. Lafayette St.
BEAUTY PARLORS
Service, 840 Lewis St.

GARY
HOTELS
Hotel Toledo
22nd Ave. & Adams St.
Phone: 5-2242
States', 1700 Washington St.
Hayes, 2167 Broadway
DRUG STORES
Haley's, 1600 Broadway
DRY CLEANING
Bufkin, 2472 Broadway

INDIANAPOLIS
HOTELS
Ferguson, 1102 N. Capitol Ave.
Y.M.C.A., 450 N. Senate Ave.
Y.W.C.A., 653 N. West St.
Hawaii, 406 Indiana Ave.
Harbour, 617-19 N. Ill. St.
Marquis, 406 Indiana Ave.
Severin, 201 So. Illinois Ave.
TOURIST HOMES
Estelle, 455 W. 10th St.
RESTAURANTS
Lasley's, 510 Indiana Ave.
Parkview, 321 N. California Ave.
Log Cabin, 524 Indiana Ave.
Taylor's, 427 W. Mich. St.
Westmorland, 1309 E. 15th St.
Blue Eagle, 648 Indiana Ave.
Courtesy, 1217 Senate St.
Perkins, 793 Indiana Ave.
BEAUTY PARLORS
Burgess, 909 W. 29th St.
Beauty Box, 2704 Clifton St.
Dancy's, 436 N. California Ave.
Mignor's, 2457 Northwestern Sun
Home Beauty Parlor, 2704 Clifton St.
Majorette, 1509 E. 25th St.
Fannie Bowles, 418 W. 28th St.
Campbell, 2439 N. Western Ave.
Noonie's, 547 N. Senate Ave.

26

Crawford's, 450 Blake St.
Home Beauty Shop, 2704 Clifton
St.
Terry's, 233 Indiana Ave.
Mary Childs, 721 Indiana Ave.
TAVERNS
Downbeat, 977 Indiana Ave.
Mayes Cafe, 503 Indiana
Ritz, Sinate & Indiana
Sunset, 875 Indiana
M. C., 544 W. Maryland St.
Panama, 306 Indiana
Downbeat, 1005 Indiana Ave.
Andrew Perkins, 793 Indiana Ave.
Glenn's Place, 1771 Boulevard Pl.
Sunset, 875 Indiana Ave.
Cassa De Amor, 924 N. W. St.
CAFES
Sugar Bowl, 952 N. West St.
SERVICE STATIONS
Al's Auto Laundry, Mich. & Blake
Sts.
GARAGES
25th St. Garage, 560 W. 25th St.
DRUG STORES
Ethical, 628 Indiana Ave.
TAILORS
Lee's, 401 W. 29th St.
Meyer O. Jacobs, 212-214 E. 16th St.
Leon, 235 Mass. Ave.
LIQUOR STORES
Anna Bell's, 956 N. W. St.
Park Package, 1320 E. 25th St.
799 Liq. Store, 799 Indiana Ave.
Little Chum, 1422 N. Capitol Ave.
Avenue Liquor, 402 Indiana Ave.
Jimmy's, Cor. Blackford & New
York St.
Steve's, 747 W. New York St.
Carl's, 2817 Clifton
NIGHT CLUBS
Savoy, 25th & Martendale
Blue Bird Inn, 502 Agnes St.
Blue Eagle Inn, 648 Indiana Ave.

JEFFERSONVILLE
TOURIST HOMES
Charles Thomas, 607 Missouri Ave.

MARION
TOURIST HOMES
Mrs. Violet Rhinehardt, 425 W. 10th
Mrs. Albert Ward, 324 W. 14th St.
RESTAURANT
Custer's Last Stand
State Rts. 15 & 37
Marshal's, 414-418 E. 4th St.
SERVICE STATION
Dave's, 2nd & By Pass

KOKOMO
TOURIST HOMES
Mrs. C. W. Winburn, 1015 Kennedy
St.
Mrs. Charles Hardinson, 812 Kennedy St.
Mrs. S. D. Hughes, 1045 N. Kennedy St.

MICHIGAN CITY
TOURIST HOMES
Allen's, 210 E. 2nd St.

MUNICE
HOTELS
Y.M.C.A., 9065 Madison

SOUTH BEND
RESTAURANTS
Smokes, 432 S. Chapin St.

TERRE HAUTE
HOTELS
Booker, 33½ No. 3rd St.
Booker, 306 Cherry St.

WEST BADEN SPRINGS
HOTELS
Waddy

IOWA

CEDAR RAPIDS
TOURIST HOMES
Brown's, 818 9th Ave. S. E.

DES MOINES
HOTELS
Y.W.C.A., 512 9th St.
La Marguerita, 1425 Center St.
RESTAURANTS
Sampson, 1246 E. 17th St.
Cunningham's, 1602 E. University
Ida Bell's, 783 11th St.
Gertrudes, 1308 Keo Way
Peck's, 1180 13th St.
Community, 1202 Center St.
Ida Bell's, 783 Eleventh
Buzz Inn, 1006 Center St.
Erma & Carrie's, 1908 Center St.
William's, 1200 East 16th St.
BEAUTY PARLORS
Miniature, 1145 Enos
Vo-Pon, 1656 Walker St.
Berlin, 1022 13th St.
Polly's, 1544 Walker St.
Evalon, 1206 Center St.
Bernice's, 911 W. 16th St.
Miniature, 1145 Enis St.
Ruth's, 905 Laurel St.
TAVERNS
Herb's, 1002 Center St.
SERVICE STATIONS
Eagle, 2246 Hubble Blvd.
Mumford's, 4th & Euclid Ave.

27

GARAGES
4th St. 417 4th St.
TAILORS
National, 808 12th St.
Clean Craft, 1300 6th Ave.
DRUG STORES
Adams, E. 5th & Locust St.

DUBUQUE
TOURIST HOMES
Mrs. P. Martin, 712 University Ave.
Mrs. Edwin Weaver, 795 Roberts Ave.

KEOKUK
CAFES
Bradley's Blessed Mart in Cafe 1103 Main St.

OTTUMWA
TOURIST HOMES
William Bailey, 526 Center Ave.
Harry Owens, 814 W. Pershing

SIOUX CITY
RESTAURANTS
Prince Henry, 704 W. 7th St.
BEAUTY PARLORS
Fannie Mae's, 611 Cook St.

WATERLOO
TOURIST HOMES
Mrs. B. F. Tredwell, 928 Beach St.
Mrs. Spencer, 220 Summer St.
Mrs. E. Lee, 745 Vinton St.

KANSAS

ATCHISON
TOURIST HOMES
Mrs. M. McDonald, 1001 So. 7th St.
Mrs. Geneva Miles, 924 N. 9th St.

BETHEL
COUNTRY CLUB
Penrod, R. F. D. 1

COFFEYVILLE
TOURIST HOMES
Roberts Rooms, 8 E. 5th St.

CONCORDIA
TOURIST HOMES
Mrs. B. Johnson, 102 E. 2nd St.
Mrs. Glen McVey, 328 East St.

EMPORIA
TOURIST HOMES
Elliott's, 816 Congress St.

EDWARSVILLE
TOURIST HOMES
Road House, Anderson's Highway 32 & Bitts Creek

FORT SCOTT
HOTELS
Hall's, 223½ E. Wall St.

HIAWATHA
TOURIST HOMES
Mrs. Mary Sanders, 1014 Shawnee

HUTCHINSON
TOURIST HOMES
Mrs. C. Lewis, 400 W. Sherman

JUNCTION CITY
HOTELS
Bridgeforth, 311 E. 11th St.
TOURIST HOMES
Mrs. B. Jones, 229 E. 14th St.

LARNED
TOURIST HOMES
Mrs. C. M. Madison, 828 W. 12th St.
Mrs. Mose Madison, 815 W. 16th St.
Mrs. John Caro, 218 E. 4th St.
RESTAURANTS
Carrie's Bar-B-Q, 218 E. 4th St.

LAURENCE
HOTELS
Snowden's, 1933 Tennessee St.

LEAVENWORTH
TOURIST HOMES
Mrs. W. Shelton, 216 Poplar St.

KANSAS CITY
RESTAURANT
Keystone Club, 4th & Freemen
BARBER SHOPS
Dabb's, 10th & Oakland
BEAUTY PARLORS
Sander's, 1813 N. 5th St.
ROAD HOUSES
De Moss, 44th & Sorta Rd., Rt. 3
GARAGES
Economy, 1935 N. 5th St.
Arthur's, 2414 N. 5th St.
DRUG STORES
Whitney's, 5th & Virginia
Cundiff, 5th & Quindarf

MANHATTAN
MOTEL
George's, 826 Tuma St.
TOUIST HOMES
Mrs. E. Dawson, 1010 Yuma St.

OTTAWA
TOURIST HOMES
Mrs. H. W. White, 821 Cypress

TOPEKA

HOTELS
Dunbar, 400 Quincy St.
Palma House, 313 Quincy St.
TOURIST HOMES
Mrs. E. Slaughter, 1407 Monroe
RESTAURANTS
Jenkins, 112 East 4th St.
Blue Heaven, 301 E. 1st St.
Joe Andy's, 1000 Washington St.
BARBER SHOPS
Lytle's, 107 E. 4th St.
Power's, 402 Quincy St.
BEAUTY PARLORS
Newton's, 1316 Van Buren St.
Avalia's, 1800 Van Buren St.
TAVERNS
Macks', 400 Quincy St.
SERVICE STATIONS
Powers, 401 Quincy St.

WICHITA

TOURIST HOMES
Mrs. E. Reed, 517½ N. Main St.
BEAUTY PARLORS
Veluntex, 532 Wabash Ave.
RESTAURANTS
Oklahoma Cafe, 517 N. Main St.
DRUG STORES
Jackson's, 1411 N. Hydraulic

KENTUCKY
BOWLING GREEN

NANCY'S TEA ROOM
Good Food Served Right

Dinners - Short Orders - Sandwiches
½ Block off 31W - Open 6 A.M.
NANCY BROWN, *Proprietor*
415 THIRD STREET
Bowling Green, Ky.   Tel. 5233

ELIZABETHTOWN
TOURIST HOMES
A. Johnson, Valley Creek Rd.
Mrs. B. Tyler, Mile St.

HAZARD
TOURIST HOMES
Mrs. J. Razor, 436 E. Main St.

HOPKINSVILLE
TOURIST HOMES
Mrs. E. Davis, 901 E. Hayes St.
L. McNary, 113 Liberty St.
J. C. Hopkins, 128 Liberty St.

LANCASTER
TOURIST HOMES
Burn's, Buford St.
Hord's, Buford St.

RESTAURANTS
Plum's, Buford St.
BEAUTY PARLORS
Hilltop, Buford St.
GARAGES
Warren & Francis, N. Campbell St.

LINCOLN RIDGE
TOURIST HOMES
Lincoln Institute

LOUISVILLE
HOTELS
Brown's Guest House
1121 W. Chestnut St.
Allen, 2516 W. Madison St.
Y.W.C.A., 528 S. 6th St.
Y.M.C.A., 920 W. Chestnut St.
TOURIST HOMES
Brown's, 1121 W. Chestnut St.
RESTAURANTS
Jones Chicken Shack
525 South 13th St.
Jones, 525 So. 13th St.
Brown Derby, 563 So. 10th St.
Betty's Grill, 547 So. 9th St.
Sara's, 1617 W. Jefferson St.
Miller's, 630 W. Walnut St.
Sally's, 1104 W. Walnut St.
Paddock, 617 So. 24th St.
Eatmore, 964 S. 12th St.
Harry's, 28th & Chestnut Sts.
Pedra's, 619 Walnut St.
Kelman's, 1832 Magazine St.
DRIVE IN
Jones Bar-B-Q, 771 S. Clay St.
BEAUTY PARLORS
Elizabeth's, 1200 W. Kentucky
Scotty's, 442 So. 21st St.
Bellonia, 1625 Callagher St.
Jones, 409 S. 18th St.
Va's, 221 S. 28th St.
Beauty Box, 922 W. Walnut St.
Rose's, 1813 W. Walnut St.
Willie's, 1815 W. Madison St.
Lov-Lee, Ladies, 529 S. 12th St.
Va's, 221 So. 28th St.
BARBER SHOPS
Hunter's, 1502 W. Chestnut St.
Miller's, 818 W. Walnut St.
TAVERNS
Herman, 1601 W. Walnut St.
Dave's, 13th & Magazine
Shiek's, 12th & Zane St.
NIGHT CLUBS
Top-Hat, 1210 W. Walnut St.
ROAD HOUSES
LIQUOR STORES
Palace, 12th & Walnut St.
Lyons, 16th & Walnut St.
GARAGES
Eade's, 3509 Dumesril
Lone Wolf, 1500 Garland Ave.

SERVICE STATIONS
F. & M. 8th and Walnut St.
DRUG STORES
Camers, 18th & Broadway
TAXI CABS
Lincoln, 705 W. Walnut
Dependable, 1835 W. Walnut St.

PARIS
RESTAURANTS
Webster's, 112 W. 8th St.
BARBER SHOPS
Webster, 110 W. 8th St.
BEAUTY PARLORS
Robinson, Lilleston St.

PADUCAH
HOTELS
Metropolitan House
724 Jackson St.
Jefferson, 514 So. 8th St.
Metropolitan, 724 Jackson St.

LEXINGTON
TOURIST HOMES
Mrs. K. Wallace, 600 W. Maxwell

LOUISIANA

BATON ROUGE
HOTELS
Ever-Ready, 1325 Government St.
TOURIST HOMES
T. Harrison, 1236 Louisiana Ave.
RESTAURANTS
Ideal Cafeteria, 1501 E. Blvd.
TAVERNS
Waldo's, 712 Peach St.
BEAUTY PARLORS
Carrie's, 561 S. 13th St.
SERVICE STATIONS
Horatio's Esso, No. 1, 1150 South St.
Horatio's Esso, No. 3, 1607 Govt. St.
ROAD HOUSE
Apex, 978 Louise St.

BOGALUSA
TOURIST HOMES

LAFAYETTE
TOURIST HOMES
Bourges, 416 Washington St.

LAKE CHARLES
HOTELS
Lewis, 515 Boulevard
TOURIST HOME
Combre's Place, 601 Boulevard

LAKE PROVIDENCE
SERVICE STATIONS
Armstrong's, 817 Sparrow St.

MANSFIELD
TOURIST HOMES
W. Simpkins, Jenkins St.

MONROE
HOTELS
Turner, 1015 Desiard St.
Dudley's Hotel, 1015 Desiard St.
RESTAURANTS
Red Union, 705½ Desiard

MORGAN CITY
TOURIST HOMES
Mrs. L. Williams, 719 Federal Ave.
Mrs. V. Williams, 208 Union St.

MARREO
BEAUTY PARLORS
Shirley, 101 Robertson Ave.

NEW ORLEANS
HOTELS
Creole Ritz, 1314 Varondelet St.
Hotel Foster, 2926 LaSalle St.
Patterson's, 802½ S. Rampart St.
Vogue, 2231 Thalia St.
North Side, 1513 La Harpe St.
Gladstone, 3435 Dryades St.
Astoria, 235 S. Rampart St.
Paige, 1035 Dryades Ave.
Riley, 759 S. Rampart St.
New Roxy, 759 S. Rampart St.
Golden Leaf, 1209 Saratoga St.
Caldonia Inn, St. Claude & St. Phillip
TOURIST HOMES
Mrs. J. Montgomery, 2134 Harmony St.
Mrs. F. Livaudais, 1954 Jackson
N. J. Bailey, 2426 Jackson Ave.
Mrs. King, 2826 Louisiana Ave.
Mrs. Edgar Major, 2739 Jackson Ave.
RESTAURANTS
Honey Dew Inn, 115 Front St.
Place-of-Joy, 2700 Melpomene St.
Dooky, Cor. Orleans & Miro
Foster's Chicken Den, Cor. LaSalle & 7th St.
Hayes Chicken Shack, La. & Saratoga St.
Portia's, 2426 Louisiana Ave.
Gumbo House, 1936 La, Ave.
BARBER SHOPS
Lopez's, 447 S. Rampart St.
BEAUTY PARLORS
Bessie's, 1841 St. Ann St.
Ola's, 1320 St. Bernard Ave.
BEAUTY CULTURE SCHOOLS
Poro, 2217 Dryades St.
TAVERNS
Di Leo, 3911 Fairmont
Wonder Bar, 2304 London Ave.
Astoria, 235 S. Rampart St.
Club Crystal, 1601 Dumaine

30

Le Rendez-vous, 7 Mile Post Gent-
    itly Highway
Horseshoe, Thalia & S. Rampart St.
Robin Hood, 2069 Jackson Ave.
Caldonia Inn, St. Phillips & Claude
    Ave.
Martin's, 1341 St. Anthony St.
Robin Hood, 2140 Loyla St.
NIGHT CLUBS
Dew Drop Inn, 2836 La Salle St.
Shadowland, 1921 Washington Ave.
Hi-Hat, N. Villere at St. Ann
Deside, 2604 Desire St.
Dileo, 3911 Fairmont Dr.
Caldonia Inn, St. Claude & St.
    Phillip Sts.
Bradshaw Wonder Bar, 2440 London
    Ave.
SERVICE STATIONS
Bill Board, 2900 Claiborne Ave.
Ross, 1330 S. Broad St.
TAXI CABS
Ed's, 315 S. Rampart St.
V-8 Cab Line, Felicity & Howard
    Sts.
Logan, 2730 Felicity St.

NEW IBERIA
TOURIST HOMES
M. Robertson, 116 Hopkins St.
N. E. Cooper, 913 Providence St.

OPELCUSAS
TOURIST HOMES
B. Giron, S. Lombard St.

SCOTLANDVILLE
SERVICE STATIONS
Horatio's Esso No. 2, Hiway 61

SHREVEPORT
TOURIST HOMES
Mrs. Ed. Turner, 309 Douglas St.
Mrs. J. Jones, 1950 Hotchkiss
Mrs. W. Elder, 1920 Hotchkiss

RESTAURANTS
Wilson's, 840 Williamson St.
Grand Terrace, Pierre & Looney St.
TAVERNS
Grand Terrace, Pierre Ave. at
    Looney
New Tuxedo, 611 East 70th St.
SERVICE STATIONS
Pat's, Milam at Lawrence St.
Ross', 901 Pierre St.
William's-Milan & Ross-Milan
    Ave.
BARBER SHOPS
Clay's, 1017 Texas Ave.
TAILORS
3 Way, 2415 Milam St.
Sprague St., 1459 Murphy St.
DRUG STORES
Peoples, 912 Pierre St.
New Avenue, 1062 Texas Ave.
LIQUOR STORES
Dandy, 918 Harwell St.

WASHINGTON
SERVICE STATIONS
Stephen's, Main St.

MAINE

GARDNIER
TOURIST HOMES
Pond View, Pleasant Pond Rd.

OLD ORCHARD
TOURIST HOMES
Mrs. R. Cumming's, 110 Portland
    Ave.

AUGUSTA
TOURIST HOMES
Mrs. Joseph McLean, 16 Drew St.

PORTLAND
TOURIST HOMES
Thomas House, 28 'A' St.

31

MARYLAND

ANNAPOLIS
RESTAURANTS
Alsop's, Northwest & Calvert Sts.

BALTIMORE
BARBER SHOPS
Scotty's, 1501 Penna. Ave.
Goldsborough, 524 Bloom St.
HOTELS
York, 1200 Madison Ave.
Smith's, Druid Hill Ave. & Paca St.
Majestic, 1602 McCulloh St.
Y.W.C.A., 1916 Madison Ave.
Honor Reed, 667 N. Franklin
Y.M.C.A., 1617 Druid Hill Ave.
TOURIST HOMES
Mrs. E. Watsons, 340 Blura St.
RESTAURANTS
Sphinx, 2107 Pennsylvania Ave.
Upton, Cor. Monroe & Edmondson
Sess, 1639 Division St.
G. & L., Fayette & Gilmore Sts
Spot Bar-B-Q, 1530 Penna Ave.
Club Barbeque, 1519 Penna. Ave.
BEAUTY PARLORS
M. King, 1510 Penna. Ave.
Scott's, 1526 Penna. Ave.
Young's, 613 W. Lafayette Ave.
La Blanche, 1531 Penna. Ave.
TAVERNS
Sugar Hill, 2361 Druid Hill Ave.
Velma, Cor. Penn & Baker St.
The Alhambra, 1520 Penna. Ave.
Gamby's, 1504 Penna. Ave.
Mayflower, 905 Madison Ave.
Dixie, 558 Baker St.
Frolic, 1401 Penna. Ave.
NIGHT CLUBS
Little Comedy, 1414 Penn Ave.
Ubangi, 2213 Penna. Ave.
Wonderland, 2043 Penna.
Gambie's, 1502 Penna. Ave.
Casino, 1517 Penna. Ave.
ROAD HOUSES
Bertie's, 2432 Annapolis Ave.
LIQUOR STORES
D. & D, 890, Linden Ave.
Fine's, 1817 Penna. Ave.
Hackerman's, 1733 Penna.
SERVICE STATIONS
Esso-Presstman & Fremont
GARAGES
Service, 1415 Etting St.

BOWIE
HOTELS
Stephens Bowie, Bowie-Laurel Rd.

CUMBERLAND
TOURIST HOMES
Glennwood Manor, 927 Glenwood St.

GLENBURNE
DRIVE INN
Brook's, 113 Crainway N. E.,
Rt. 301

FREDERICK
TOURIST HOMES
Mrs. J. Makel, 119 E. 5th St.
Mrs. W. W. Roberts, 316 W. South
RESTAURANTS
Crescent, 16 W. All Saint St.

HAGERSTOWN
TOURIST HOMES
Harmon, 226 N. Jonathan St.
RESTAURANTS
Ship Tea Room, 329 N. Jonathan St.

HAVRE DE GRACE
HOTELS
Johnson's, 415 S. Stokes St.

PRINCESS ANNE
RESTAURANTS
Victory, 137 Broad St.

TURNERS STATION
NIGHT CLUBS
Adam's
DRUG STORES
Balnew's, 101 Sollers Pt. Rd.

UPPER MARLBORO
HOTELS
Midway

WALDORF
RESTAURANTS
Blue Bird Inn

MASSACHUSETTS

ATTLEBORO
TOURIST HOMES
J. R. Brooks, Jr., 54 James St.

BOSTON
HOTELS
Mothers Lunch, 510 Columbia Ave.
Lucille, 52 Rutland Sq.
Harrett Tubman, 25 Holyoke St.
Columbus Arms, 455 Columbus Ave.
TOURIST HOMES
Julia Walters, 912 Fremont
Holeman, 212 W. Springfield St.
M. Johnson, 616 Columbus Ave.
Mrs. E. A. Taylor, 192 W. Springfield St.
Guest House, 191 Humbolt St.
Randolph House, 153 Worcester St.
Mrs. P. J. Reynolds, 613 Columbus Ave.
Smith's, 14 Yarmouth St.
RESTAURANTS
Edyth's, 170 W. Springfield St.
Slades, 958 Tremont St.
Charlie's, 429 Columbus Ave.
Sunnyside, 411 Columbus Ave.
Western, 415 Mass. Ave.
Estelles, 888 Tremont St.

BEAUTY PARLORS
Mme. F. S. Blake, 363 Mass. Ave.
E. L. Crosby, 11 Greenwich Park
Mme. Enslow's, 977 Tremont St.
W. Milliams, 62 Hammond St.
E. West, 609 Columbus Ave.
House of Charms, 169-A W. Springfield
Josephine Bolt, 374 Columbus Ave.
Ruth Evans, 563 Columbus Ave.
Rubinetta, 961 Tremont St.
Lucile's, 226 W. Springfield St.
Constance, 414 Mass. Ave.
Easter's, 168A Springfield St.
Arizona, 563 Columbus Ave.
Betty's, 609 Columbus Ave.
Clark-Merrill, 567 Shawmut Ave.
Amy's, 782 Tremont St.
Doris, 767 Tremont St.
La Newton, 462 Mass. Ave.
Belleza De La Casa, 360 Mass. Ave.
BARBER SHOPS
Amity, 1028 Tremont St.
Abbott's, 974 Tremont St.
NIGHT CLUBS
Savoy, 410 Mass. Ave.
TAVERNS
4-H Lounge, 411 Columbus Ave.
TAILORS
Baltimore, 1013 Tremont St.
Chester's, 189 W. Newton St.

CAMBRIDGE
TOURIST HOMES
Mrs. S. P. Bennett, 26 Mead St.

EVERETT
BEAUTY PARLORS
Ruth's, 20 Woodward St.

GREAT BARRINGTON
TOURIST HOMES
Mrs. I. Anderson, 28 Rossiter St.
Mrs. J. Hamilton, 118 Main St.
Crawford's Inn, 14 Elm Court

HYAMIS
TOURIST HOMES
Zilphas Cottages, 134 Oakneck Rd.

NORTH ADAMS
TOURIST HOMES
F. Adams, 32 Washington Ave.

NORTH CAMBRIDGE
TOURIST HOMES
Mrs. L. G. Hill, 39 Hubbard Ave.

NEEDHAM
TOURIST HOMES
B. Chapman, 789 Central Ave.

PITTSFIELD
TOURIST HOMES
M. E. Grant, 53 King St.
Mrs. T. Dillard, 109 Linden St.
J. Marshall, 124 Danforth Ave.

RANDOLPH
RESTAURANTS
Mary Lee Chicken Shack, 482 Main St.

ROXBURY
BEAUTY PARLORS
Ruth E. Colery's, 132 Warren St.
Janett's, 132 Humboldt Ave.
Charm Grove, 96 Humboldt St.
Mme. Lovett, 68 Humboldt St.
Belinda's, 429 Shawmut Ave.
Cherrie Charm Cove, 90 Humboldt Ave.
Mae's, 140 Lenox St.
Lovett's, 69 Humboldt Ave.
Ruth's, 185 Warren St.
BARBER SHOPS
Wright's, 51A Humboldt St.
Metropolitan, Ruggles & Ashburn Sts.
SERVICE STATIONS
Thompson's, 1105 Tremont St.
Atlanta, 1105 Tremont St.
TAILORS
Morgan's, 355 Warren St.
DRUG STORES
Douglas Square, 1002 Tremont St.
Jaspan's, 134 Harold St.
Kornfield's, 2121 Washington St.

SOUTH HANSON
TOURIST HOMES
Modern, 26 Reed St.

SPRINGFIELD
HOTELS
Springfield
BARBER SHOPS
Joiner's, 97 Hancock St.
BEAUTY PARLORS
Mrs. Law's, 18 Hawley St.
TAILORS
American Cleaners, 433 Eastern Ave.

SWAMPSCOTT
TOURIST HOMES
Mrs. M. Home, 3 Boynton St.

WOBURN
TOURIST HOMES
Mrs. A. E. Roberts, 128 Dragon Ct.

WORCESTER
HOTELS
Worcester, Washington Square
SERVICE STATIONS
Kozarian's, 53 Summer St.
GARAGES
Bancroft, 24 Portland St.
DRUG STORES
Bergwall, 238 Main St.

MICHIGAN

ANN ARBOR
HOTELS
American, 123 Washington St.
Allenel, 126 El Huron St.

BATTLE CREEK
TOURIST HOMES
Mrs. F. Brown, 76 Walters Ave.

BALDWIN
LODGES
Teresa's, Rt. 1
TOURIST HOMES
Whip-or-Will Cottage, Rt. No. 1,
Box 178B
NIGHT CLUBS
El Morocco

BENTON HARBOR
NIGHT CLUBS
Research Pleasure Club, 362 8th St.

BITELY
HOTELS
Royal Breeze, Woodland Park

KELSONIA INN
Enjoy the Country, Air, Swimming &
Boating - Cottages by the Week
or Month - Rooms, Modern
Conveniences
Get Good Food - How You Want It
For Res., phone Baldwin 37F21
Woodland Pk. Resort   Bitely, Mich.
Roscoe C. Terry, *Proprietor*

NEW BUFFALO
RESTAURANTS
Fire Side, U. S. Rt. 12

COVERT
HOTELS
Star

DETROIT
HOTELS
Capitol, 114 East Palmer
McGraw, 5605 Junction St.
Gotham, 111 Orchestra Place
Mark Twain, E. Garfield & Wood-
ward
Biltmore, 1926 St. Antoine St.
Elizabeth, 413 E. Elizabeth St.
Fox, 715 Madison St.
Norwood, 550 E. Adams St.
Russell, 615 E. Adams St.
Touraine, 4614 John R. St.
Terraine, John R. & Garfield
Northcross, 2205 St. Antoine
Dewey, 595 E. Adams St.
Davidson, 556 E. Forest Ave.
Edenburgh, 758 Westchester Ave.
Old Rivers, 2036 Hastings
Sportman's, 3767 W. Warren Ave.
Carlton Plaza, John R at Edmund

Paradise, 710 Madison St.
Ebony, 110 Chandler St.
Summers, 412 Frederick St.
Australian, 5464 Rivard
TOURIST HOMES
Labland, 39 Orchestra Place
RESTAURANTS
Pelican, 4613 John R. St.
BEAUTY SCHOOLS
Bee-Dew, 703 E. Forest Ave.
Hair Health, 1332 Gratiot Ave.
BARBER SHOPS
Swanson's, 3415 Hastings St.
Arcade, Hastings & Napoleon
Universal, 3129 Hastings St.
TAVERNS
Champion, Oakland & Holbrook
Horseshoe, 666 Club
Broad's, 8825 Oakland
Herman's, 3458 Buchanan
Flame, 4264 John R. St.
Bizerte, 9006 Oakland
Frolic, 4450 John R. St.
Royal Blue, 8401 Russell
NIGHT CLUBS
Congo, 2337 Gratiot St.
Uncle Tom's, 8206 W. 8 Mile Rd.
SERVICE STATIONS
Johnson's, McGraw & 25th St.
Cobb's, Maple & Chene Sts.
Homer's, 589 Madison Ave.
AUTOMOBILES
Davis Motor Co., 421 E. Vernon
Highway
TAILORS
Kenilworth, 131 Kenilworth
Blair, 277 Gratiot St.
DRUG STORES
Clay, Clay & Cameron Ave.
Kay, 4766 McGraw Ave.

FLINT
TOURIST HOMES
T. L. Wheeler, 1512 Liberty St.
Mrs. F. Taylor, 1615 Clifford St.

GRAND JUNCTION
TOURIST HOMES
Hamilton Farms, RFD No. 1

IDLEWILD
HOTELS
Lydia Inn, Box 81
Casa Blanca
Oakmere
Paradise Gardens
McKnight's
Phil Giles
Club El Morocco, Rt. No. 1, Box
TOURIST HOMES
Edinburgh Cottage, Miss Herrone
B. Riddles
Rainbow Manor
Douglas Manor
Bash Inn, B'way at Hemlock
Spizerinktom
Rest Haven

34

RESTAURANTS
Rosanna's
Whiteway Inn
Navajo
TAVERNS
Rosana
Purple Palace
Paradise Gardens
JACKSON
TOURIST HOMES
Mrs. W. Harrison, 1215 Greenwood Ave.
LANSING
TOURIST HOMES
Mrs. M. Gray, 1216 St. Joseph St.
Mrs Lewis, 816 S. Butler St.
Mrs. Gaines, 1406 Albert St.
LAWRENCE
TOURIST HOMES
Flora Giles Farm
MUSKEGON
TOURIST HOMES
R. C. Merrick, 65 E. Muskegon Ave.
OSCODA
TOURIST HOMES
Jesse Colbath, Van Eten Lake
SAGINAW
TOURIST HOMES
Mrs. J. Curtley, 439 N. Third St.
SOUTH HAVEN
TOURIST HOMES
Mrs. M. Johnson, Shady Nook Farm
VANDALIA
HOTELS
Hill's Hotel, Rt. No. 1
TOURIST HOMES
Mrs. Mayme Cooper, P. O. Box 96
THREE RIVERS
TOURIST HOMES
Jordan's, Route No. 2
NILES
TOURIST HOMES
Jones Place, Rt. No. 2, Box 227..

MINNESOTA
MINNEAPOLIS
HOTELS
Serville, 246½ 4th Ave.
Golden West, 307 Wash. Ave. S.
TOURIST HOMES
Phyllis Wheatley House, 809 N. Aldrich Ave.
RESTAURANTS
Bells Cafe, 207 South 3rd St.
TAVERNS
North Side, 1011 Olson H'way
LIQUOR STORES
Walston's, 28 South 6th St.
Harold's, 619 Marq Ave.

Safro, 236 3rd Ave. So.
Mac's, 119 Washington Ave. So.
Labrie's, 324 Plymouth Ave. So.
Cook's, 239 Cedar Ave.
SERVICE STATIONS
Dirk's, 2921 5th Ave. S.
TAILORS
Ann's, 919 7th St. No.
Franklin, 3510 Cedar Ave.
MOTLEY
TOURIST HOMES
Motley's Camp
RESTAURANTS
Herman Stelcks
SERVICE STATIONS
Geo. Thorn
ROCHESTER
HOTELS
Avalon, 303 North Broadway
ST. CLOUD
HOTELS
Grand Central, 5th & St. Germaine
RESTAURANTS
Spaniol, 13 6th Ave. N.
ST. PAUL
TOURIST HOMES
Villa Wilson, 697 St. Anthony Ave.
RESTAURANTS
G. & G. Bar-B-Q, 291 No. St. Albans
Jim's, St. Anthony and Kent
SERVICE STATIONS
Gardner's, Western and Central
GARAGES
Milligan's, 1008 Rondo Ave.
TAILORS
Drew, 1597 University Ave.
LIQUOR STORES
Bond, 471 Wabasha
First, Robert at Fifth
Commerce, 2163 Ford Parkway
Seven Corners, 158 West 7th St.
St. Paul's, 200 East 7th St.
Rite, 442 Wabasha
Jack's, 517 Wabasha

MISSISSIPPI
BILOXI
TOURIST HOMES
Mrs. G. Bess, 630 Main St.
Mrs. A. J. Alcina, 443 Washington
D'LO
SERVICE STATIONS
Dades, Hi'Way 49 So.
CANTON
RESTAURANTS
Tolliver's, 115 N. Hickory
NIGHT CLUBS
Blue Garden, 5 Liberty St.
CLEVELAND
SERVICE STATIONS
7-11, Highway 61 at 8

COLUMBUS

HOTELS
Queen City, 15th St. & 7th Ave.
TOURIST HOMES
M. J. Harrison, 915 N. 14th St.
H. Sommerville, 906 N. 14th St.
Mrs. I. Roberts, 12th & 5th Ave. N.
Mrs. Chevis, 1425 11th Ave. N.

GREENVILLE

SERVICE STATIONS
Peoples, Nelson & Eddie St.

GRENADA

TOURIST HOMES
Mrs. K. D. Fisher, 72 Adams St.
F. Williams, H'way 51 & Fairground Rd.
Mrs. Leola C. Fisher, 700 Govan St.

HATTIESBURG

TOURIST HOMES
W. A. Godbolt, 409 E. 7th St.
Mrs. A. Crosby, 413 E. 6th St.
Mrs. S. Vann, 636 Mobile St.

JACKSON

HOTELS
Summers Hotel, 619 W. Pearl St.
Edward Lee, 144 W. Church St.
RESTAURANTS
Shepherds Kitchenette, 604 N. Farish
TOURIST HOMES
Wilson House, 154 W. Oakley St.
BEAUTY PARLORS
Davis Salon, 703 N. Farish St.
BARBER SHOPS
City, 127 N. Farish St.
TAILORS
Paris, 800 N. Parish St.

DRUG STORES
Palace, 504 N. Farish St.
SERVICE STATIONS
Johnson's, 536 N. Farish
GARAGES
Farish St., 752 N. Farish
TAXI CABS
Veterans, 116 W. Amite St.

LAUREL

HOTELS
Bass, S. Pine St.
TOURIST HOMES
Mrs. E. L. Brown, 522 E. Kingston
Mrs. S. G. Wilson, 802 S. 7th

MACOMB

TOURIST HOMES
D. Mason, 218 Denwidde St.

MENDENHALL

SERVICE STATIONS
Bob's, H'way 49
Smith's, Hi'way 49 No.

MERIDIAN

HOTELS
E. F. Young, 500 25th St.
Beales, 2411 Fifth St.
TOURIST HOMES
C. W. Williams, 1208 31st St.
Mrs. M. Simmons, 5th St. betw. 16 & 17 Ave.
Charley Leigh, 5th St. & 16th Ave.

MOUND BAYOU

TOURIST HOMES
Mrs. Sallie Price
Mrs. Charlotte Strong
GARAGES
Liddle's

NEW ALBANY
HOTELS
Foot's, Railroad Ave.
TOURIST HOMES
S. Drewery, Church St.

PASSAGOULA
TOURIST HOMES
Mrs. Minnie B. Wilson, 1001 Kenneth Ave.

YAZOO CITY
HOTELS
Caldwell, Water & Broadway Sts.
TOURIST HOMES
Mrs. A. J. Walker, 321 S. Monroe

MISSOURI

CAPE GIRADEAU
TOURIST HOMES
W. Martin, 38 N. Hanover St.
J. Randol, 422 North St.

COLUMBIA
HOTELS
Austin House, 108 E. Walnut St.
TOURIST HOMES
Mrs. W. Harvey, 417 N. 3rd St.
E. Williams, 314 McBain St.
Williams' Home, 223 Lynn St.
BEAUTY PARLOR
Buckner's Beauty Shop,
502 N. 3rd St.

CHARLESTON
TAVERNS
Creole Cafe, 311 Elm St.

EXCELSIOR SPRINGS
HOTELS
The Albany, 408 South St.
Moore's, 302 Maine St.
Excelsior Springs Hotel, 302 Main St.

HANNIBAL
TOURIST HOMES
Mrs. E. Julius, 1218 Gerard St.

JEFFERSON CITY
HOTELS
Lincoln, 600 Lafayette St.
Booker T.
TOURIST HOMES
Miss C. Woodridge, 418 Adams St.
R. Graves, 314 E. Dunklin St.
RESTAURANTS
De Luxe, 601 Lafayette St.
Blue Tiger, Chestnut & E Atchenson St.
College, 905 E. Atchenson St.
BARBER SHOPS
Tayes, Elm & Lafayette Sts.
BEAUTY PARLORS
Poro, 818 Lafayette St.

TAVERNS
Tops, 626 Lafayette St.
NIGHT CLUBS
Subway, 600 Lafayette St.
Lone Star, 930 E. Miller St.
TAXI CABS
Veteran, 515 Lafayette St.
TAILORS
Rightway, 903 E. Atchenson St.

JOPLIN
TOURIST HOMES
Williams, 308 Penna. St.
J. Lindsay, 1702 Penna. St.
Mrs. F. Echols, 901 Missouri Ave.

KANSAS CITY
HOTELS
Cadillac, 1429 Forest
Booker T. Hotel, 1823 Vine St.
921 Hotel, 921 East 17th St.
Parkview, 10th & Paseo
Street's, 1510 E. 18th St.
Lincoln Hotel, 13th & Woodland Sts.
Square Deal, 1305 E. 18th St.
TOURIST HOMES
Thos. Wilson, 2600 Euclid
Y.W.C.A., 1908, The Paseo
Mrs. Vallie Lamb, 1914 E. 24th St.
RESTAURANTS
Old Kentucky's, 2401 Brooklyn
Oven, 17th & Vine St.
Elmora's Cafe, 1518 E. 18th St.
Famous, 12th & Forest
M. & T., 2013 E. 12th St.
Mim's Cafe, 1603 East 12th St.
TAVERNS
Forest Bar, 1200 E. 18th St.
Vine St., 1519 E. 12th St.
Blackhawk, 1410 E. 14th St.
Green Duck, 2548 Prospect
NIGHT CLUBS
El Capitan, 1610 E. 18th St.
BEAUTY PARLORS
Queen Ann, 1504 E. 11th St.
Hazel Graham, 1836 Vine St.
Arlene, 2409 Vine St.
Katherine's, 1024 East 19th St.
Haley's, 1521 E. 18th St.
Labell, 2614 Tracy
Queen Ann, 1504 East 11th St.
BARBER SHOPS
Ever-Ready, 1810A Vine St.
Barber Shop, 2603½ Prospect Ave.
LIQUOR STORES
Cardinal, 1515 E. 18th St.
Monarch, 2300 Prospect Ave.
Dundee, 1701 Troost
Virginia, 1601 Virginia
Golden Crown, 2218 Vine
Ace, 2404 Vine
Tracy's, 2001 Olive
Donnell, 18th & Troost Sts.
Rubin's, 19th & Vine
Donnich, 18th & Troost

SERVICE STATIONS
Mobile Station, 1502 E. 19th St.
GARAGES
DRUG STORES
Community, 2432 Vine St.
Johnson's, 2300 Vine St.
Regal's, 2462 Brooklyn Ave.
Prospect, 18th & Prospect
Truman Rd., 2133 Truman Rd.
TAILORS
Spotless, 2303 Prospect Ave.
Courtney, 1715 Brooklyn Ave.

KIMLOCK
BEAUTY PARLORS
Hall's, 659 Carson Rd.
DRUG STORES
Kimlock, Lix & Carson Rd.

MOBERLY
TOURIST HOMES
Ralph Bass, 517 Winchester St.

SEDALIA
TOURIST HOMES
Mrs. T. L. Moore, 505 W. Cooper
Mrs. C. Walker, 217 E. Morgan
W. Williams, 317 E. Johnson

ST. LOUIS
HOTELS

Once Our Guest - Always Our Guest"

BOOKER WASHINGTON
Hotel & Courts
Private Baths - Air Conditioned
Connected Garage - Radios &
Telephones in Every Room
209 N. JEFFERSON AVE.
St. Louis 3, Mo.   Tel.: JEfferson 0774

Antler, 3502, Franklin Ave.
Alcorn, 4165 Washington Ave.
Poro Hotel
4300 St. Ferdinand Ave.
West End, 3900 W. Beele St.
Grand Central, Jefferson & Pine
Calumet, 611 N. Jefferson Ave.
Midtown Hotel
2935 Lawton Ave.
Harlem, 3438 Franklin
Atlas, 4267 Delmar
Adam's, 4235 Olive St.
TOURIST HOMES
Y.W.C.A., 2709 Locust St.
RESTAURANTS
Bell's, 3867 Delmar Blvd.
DeLuxe, 10 N. Jefferson Ave.
Northside, 2422 N. Pendleton Ave.
Snack Shop, 1105 N. Taylor
Harlem Grill, 3438 Franklin
Nick's Snack House, 1109 Sarah
Wike's, 1804 N. Taylor Ave.

Ding-Ling End, 7915 Shaftsbury Ave.
Roma, 3839 Finney Ave.
Hunter's, 2610 Delmar Blvd.
Bells, 3867 Delmar Blvd.
Harlem, 3438 Franklin
BEAUTY PARLORS
Parkway, 4218 E. Moffit St.
Allen's, 2343 Market St.
Shaw's, 4256 Easton 13
Juvill, 4141 Easton 13
Young's, 2005 Pine St.
Azalie, 4716A Ashland
Amanda's, 1021 N. Cardinal Ave. 6
Boulevard, 4554 Newberry Ter.
Parkway, 4284 W. St. & Ferdinand
Montgomery, 1033 N. Compton Ave.
Harris, 919 Ohio Ave.
Marcella's, 2306 Cole St.
Tillie's, 2600 Cole St.
Long's, 3134 Bell
De Luxe, 727 Walton Ave.
M. & M., 3975 Delmar Blvd.
Argus, 1008 N. Sarah St.
Casalonia, 4067 A Easton At Sarah
Majestic, 3894 Enright Ave.
A. V's, 919 A Compton
Gloria's, 3151 Sheridan
BARBER SHOPS
Bullock's, 3320 Franklin Ave.
TAVERNS
Calumet, 759 Shaftsbury Ave.
Glass Bar, 2933 Lawson St.
Carioca, 1112½ N. Sarah St.
20th Century, 718 N. Vanderventer
West End, 939 N. Vanderventer Ave
Hawaiian, 3839 Finney Ave.
Play House, 4671 Page Blvd.
Pullman Club, 2033 Market St.
Roma, 3839 Finney Ave.
Casbah, 2605 Cass Ave.
Duck's, 4384 St. Louis Ave.
Atlas, 4267 Delmar
Bob's, 3855 Pafe Blvd.
NIGHT CLUBS
West End, 911 N. Vanderventer
Riviera, 4460 Delmar Blvd.
20th Century, 718 N. Vanderventer St.
Carioca, 112½ N. Sarah
SERVICE STATIONS
Mack's, 4067 Delmar
Midville, 1913 Pendleton Ave.
Anderson's, 930 N. Compton
Brame's, 4324A Evans
GARAGES
Garfield, 4247 Garfield
TAILORS
Jackson's, 4501 W. Easton Ave.
Orchard, 4480 Easton Ave.
LIQUOR STORES
Siegals, 3015 Locust St.
Harlem, 4161 Easton Ave.
K. & F., 215 N. Jefferson Ave.
Sid's, 1223 N. 13th St.

TAXI CABS
Blue Jay, 2811 Easton Ave.
DeLuxe, 16 N. Jefferson Ave.
DRUG STORES
Taylor Page, 4503 Easton Ave.
Williams, 2801 Cole St.
Douglas, 3339 Laclede
Harper's, 3145 Franklin
Ream's, 1319 N. Grand

RICHMOND
TOURIST HOMES
Harrison, 130 So. Hill St.

SPRINGFIELD
HOTELS

When in Springfield Stop at
ALBERTA'S HOTEL &
SNACK BAR
617 NORTH BENTON
3 blocks north of City - Route 66
ALBERTA NORTHCUTT, *Proprietor*

NEBRASKA

AINSWORTH
HOTELS
Midwest
TOURIST HOMES
Skinner's Cabins
RESTAURANTS
Top Notch
SERVICE STATIONS
Weston
Skinner's
Phillips 66
Conoco
GARAGES
House of Chevrolet
Clark's Service
Gil's Body Shop

FREMONT
Gus Henderson, 1725 N. Irving St.

LINCOLN
TOURIST HOMES
Mrs. R. E. Edwards, 2120 "I" St.
DRUG STORES
Smith's, 2146 Vine St.
TAILORS
Zimmerman, 2355 O St.

OMAHA
HOTELS
Broadview, 2060 N. 19th St.
Patton, 1014-18 S. 11th St.
Willis, 22nd & Willis
TOURIST HOMES
L. Strawther, 2220 Willis Ave.
G. H. Ashby,, 2228 Willis Ave.

TAVERNS
Myrtis, 2229 Lake St.
Len's, 23th & Q St.
Apex, 1818 N. 24th St.
LIQUOR STORES
Thrifty, 24th & Lake St.
SERVICE STATIONS
Gabby's, 24th & Ohio
Kaplan, 24th & Grant
TAILORS
Tip Top, 1804 N. 24th St.
DRUG STORES
Hermansky's, 2725 Q St.
Duffy, 24th & Lake St.
Johnson, 2306 N. 24th St.
Reid's, 24th & Seward Sts.

SCOTTSBLUFF
HOTELS
Welsh Rooms, 10th St. & 10th Ave.
TOURIST HOMES
Pickett's, Cabins, East Overland
RESTAURANTS
Eagle,'s, 1603 Broadway

NEW JERSEY

ASBURY PARK
HOTELS
Royal, 216 3rd St.
Reevy's, 135 DeWitt Ave.
Whitehad, 25 Atkins Ave.
TOURIST HOMES
Mrs. W. Greenlow, 1315 Summerfield
   Ave.
Mrs. C. Jones, 141 Sylvan Ave.
Mrs. V. Maupin, 25 Atkins Ave.
E. C. Yeager, 1406 Mattison Ave.
Anna Eaton, 23 Atkins Ave.
Mrs. Margaret Wright, 153 Sylvan
   Ave.
RESTAURANTS
Black Diamond, 106 Sylvan Ave.
West Side, 1136 Springwood Ave.
Nellie Tutt's, 1207 Springwood Ave.
BEAUTY PARLORS
Imperial, 1107 Springwood Ave.
Opal, 1146 Springwood Ave.
Marlons, 1119 Springwood Ave.
BARBER SHOPS
Consolidated, 1216 Springwood
John Milby, 1216 Springwood Ave.
TAVERNS
Capitol Tavern,
1212 Springwood Ave.
Aztex Room, 1147 Springwood Ave.
Hollywood, 1318 Springwood Ave.
2-Door, 1512 Springwood Ave.
Palm Garden, Springwood & Myrtle
   Aves.

NIGHT CLUBS
Cuba's, 1147 Springwood Ave.
SERVICE STATIONS
Johnson, Springwood & DeWitt Pl.
Bomar's, Springwood & Ridge
GARAGES
West Side, 1010 Asbury Ave.

ATLANTIC CITY

HOTELS
Bay State, N. Tenn. Ave.
Randell, 1601 Arctic Ave.
Ridley, 1806 Arctic Ave.
Wright, 1702 Arctic Ave.
Lincoln, 911 N. Indiana Ave.
Attucks, 1120 Drexel Ave.
Villanova, 1124 Drexel Ave.
Burton's, 10 No. Delaware Ave.
Johnson's, 11 N. Kentucky Ave.
Albright, 228 N. Virginia Ave.
Liberty, 1519 Baltic Ave.
TOURIST HOMES
Murphy's, 234 Virginia Ave.
Washington, 1109 Arctic Ave.
Shore, 800 Arctic Ave.
Newsome's, 225 N. Indiana Ave.
A. R. S. Goss, 324 N. Indiana Ave.
E. Satchell, 27 N. Michigan Ave.
Bailey's Cottage, 1812 Arctic Ave.
D. Austin, 813 Baltic Ave.
R. Brown, 113 N. Penn. Ave.
M. Conte, 128 N. Indiana Ave.
Burton's, 10-12 N. Delaware Ave.
Mrs. V. Jones, 1720 Arctic Ave.
Robert's, 303 No. Indiana Ave.
RESTAURANTS
J & J, 1700 Arctic Ave.
Golden's, 41 N. Kentucky Ave.
Kelly's, 1311 Arctic Ave.
BEAUTY PARLORS
C. E. Newsome, 225 N. Indiana Ave.
Grace's, 43 N. Kentucky Ave.
BARBER SHOPS
42 N. Illinois Ave.
Hollywood, 811 Arctic Ave.
Hunter's, 1816½ Arctic Ave.
TAVERNS
Mack's, 132 N. New York Ave.
Tom Buck's, 1608 Arctic Ave. ..
Lighthouse, 1605 Arctic Ave.
Wonder Bar, 1601 Arctic Ave.
Little Belmont, 37 N. Kentucky Ave.
Hattie's, 1913 Arctic Ave.
Daddy Lew's, Bay & Baltic Ave.
Popular, 1923 Arctic Ave.
Elite, Baltic & Chalfonte Ave.
Herman's, Maryland & Arctic
Prince's, 37 N. Michigan Ave.
Austin's, Maryland & Baltic
Elks Bar & Grill, 1613 Arctic
New Jersey, N. J. & Mediterranean
Circus, 37 N. Michigan Ave.
Tom Buck's, 1608 Arctic Ave.
My Own, 701 Baltic Ave.

Bill Marks, 1923 Arctic
Fannie's, 2001 Arctic Ave.
Shangri-La, Kentucky & Arctic Av.
Perry's, 1228 Arctic Ave.
Johnson's, 10 No. Kentucky Ave.
Hi-Hat, 1317 Arctic Ave.
NIGHT CLUBS
Harlem, 32 N. Kentucky Ave.
Paradise, 220 N. Illinois Ave.
LIQUOR STORES
Tumble Inn, Delaware & Baltic
SERVICE STATIONS
Mundy's, 1818 Arctic St.
DRUG STORES
London's, Cor. Ky. & Arctic Ave.

BARRINGTON

SERVICE STATIONS
Atlantic

BAYONNE

TAVERNS
John's, 463 Ave 'C'
TAILORS

BELMAR

HOTELS
Riverview, 710 8th Ave.
TOURIST HOME
Sadie's Guest House,
1304 "E" St.

BELL MEADE

HOTELS
Bell Meade, Rt. 31

BERLIN

TAVERNS
Tipping Inn, Or Rt. 841

BLOOMFIELD

RESTAURANTS
Lucy's, 376 Broughton Ave.

BRIDGETOWN

TAVERNS
The Ram's Inn, Bridgeston & Mill-
ville Pike

CAMDEN

CHINESE RESTAURANTS
Lon's, 806 Kaign Ave.
TAVERNS
Nick's, 7th & Central Ave.
TAILORS
Merchant, 743 Kaighor Ave.

CAPE MAY

HOTELS
New Cape May,
Broad & Jackson Sts.
De Griff, 83 Corgie St.
TOURIST HOMES
Mrs. B. Hillman, Johnstown Lane
Stiles, 821 Corgie St.
RESTAURANTS
Billy Boy and Lees, 220 Jackson St.

EAST ORANGE
BEAUTY PARLORS
Ritz, 214 Main St.
Milan's, 232 Halstead St.
TAILORS
Vernon's, 182 Amherst St.
Charles, 49 N. Park St.
TAXI CABS
Whitehurst, Cor. Central & Halstead St.

EATONTOWN
NIGHT CLUBS
The Greenbriar, Pine Bush

EGG HARBOR
HOTELS
Allen House, 625 Cincinnati Ave.
TAVERNS
Red, White & Blue Inn, 701 Phila. Ave.

ELIZABETH
TOURIST HOMES
Mrs. T. T. Davis, 27 Dayton
TAVERNS
One & Only, 1112 Dickerson St.
Hunter's, 1197 E. Broad St.

ENGLEWOOD
TAVERNS
The Lincoln, 1-3 Englewood Ave.
LIQUOR STORES
W. E. Beverage Co., 107 William St.
Giles, 107 William St.

HACKENSACK
BEAUTY PARLORS
Mary, 206 Central Ave.
BARBER STORES
Tip Top, 174 Central Ave.
Crosson, Railroad Place
TAVERNS
Rideout's, 204 Central Ave.
NIGHT CLUBS
Majestic Lodge, 351 1st St.
SERVICE STATIONS
Five Point, 1st & Susquehanna St.

HASKELL
RECREATION PARKS
Thomas Lake

HIGHTSTOWN
TAVERNS
Paul's Inn, Rt. 33 E. Windsor TWP
Old Barn, 104 Daws St.

JERSEY CITY
BEAUTY PARLORS
Beauty, 74A Atlantic Ave.
TAILORS
Bell's, 630 Cummunipaw Ave.
BEAUTY PARLORS
N. J. Academy, 374 Forest St.

KINGSTON
ROAD HOUSES
Merrill's

KEYPORT
TAVERNS
Green Grove Inn, Atlantic & Halsey Sts.
Major's, 215 Atlantic Ave.

KENNELWORTH
TAVERNS
Driver's, 17th & Monroe Ave.

LAWNSIDE
HOTELS
Inman, White Horse Pike
TOURIST HOMES
Hi-Hat, White Horse Pike
TAVERNS
Acorn Inn, White Horse Pike
Dreamland, Evesham Ave.
La Belle Inn, Gloucester Ave.
Wilcox, Evesham Ave.
BEAUTY PARLORS
Thelma Thomas, Warwick Blvd.
BARBER SHOPS
Henry Smith, Mouldy Rd.
RECREATION PARK
Lawnside Park
SERVICE STATIONS
Newton's, White Horse Pike

LINDEN
TAVERNS
Victory, 1305 Baltimore Ave.

LONG BRANCH
TAVERNS
Club '45', Liberty St.
Sam Hall, 180 Belmont St.
Tally-Ho, 44 Liberty St.

MADISON
TAXI CABS

MAGNOLIA
TAVERNS
Sunshine, 540 White Horse Pike

MAHWAH
TAVERNS
Paul's Lunch, Brook St.

MONMOUTH JUNCTION
TOURIST HOMES
Macon's Inn, H'way Rt. No. 1-26

MONTCLAIR
TOURIST HOMES
Y.M.C.A., 39 Washington St.
Y.W.C.A., 159 Glenridge Ave.
RESTAURANTS
Tabard's, 144 Bloomfield Ave.
Blue Front, 154 Bloomfield Ave.

BEAUTY SHOPS
Lula's, 270 Bloomfield Ave.
McGhee, 307 Orange Rd.
Gamble's, 146 Bloomfield Ave.
BARBER SHOPS
Stewart Bros., 139 Bloomfield Ave.
Walkers, 180 Bloomfield Ave.
Paramount, 215 Bloomfield Ave.
TAVERNS
Elm's, 231 Bloomfield Ave.
TAILORS
Cut Rate, 274 Bloomfield Ave.
Raveneau, 224 Bloomfield Ave.
Eay-Ayer's, 190 Bloomfield Ave.
SERVICE STATIONS
Whitefields, 175 Bloomfield Ave.
Montclairs, 170 Bloomfield Ave.
GARAGES
Cardell's, 323 Orange Rd.
Maple Ave., 91 Maple Ave.
TAXI CABS
Edmonds, 173 Bloomfield Ave.
Davenport, 152 Lincoln St.
DRUG STORES
Elm Pharmacy, 220 Bloomfield Ave.

NEPTUNE

RESTAURANTS
Hampton Inn, 1718 Springwood Ave
Samuel's, 351 Fisher Ave.
Gottlings, 118 Bradley Ave.
BEAUTY PARLORS
Priscilla's, 261 Myrtle Ave.

NEWARK

HOTELS
Rio Plaza Hotel, 92 S. 13th St.
Coleman, 59 Court St.
Grand, 78 W. Market St.
Y.M.C.A., 153 Court St.
Y.W.C.A., 20 Jones St.
Harwin Terrace, 27 Sterling St.
TOURIST HOMES
RESTAURANTS
Bar-B-Q, 9 Monmouth St.
BEAUTY PARLORS
Mae's, 161 W. Kinney St.
Wilson, 118 Springfield Ave.
La Vogue, 227 W. Kinney St.
Farrar, 35 Prince St.
Billy's, 206 Belmont Ave.
Algene's, 120 Spruce St.
Queen, 155 Barclay St.
Five-Star, 185 Kinney St.
BARBER SHOPS
El Idellio, 30 Wright St.
TAVERNS
Little Charles, 581 Central Ave.
Harlem, 109 Belmont Ave.
Howard, Springfield Ave. & Howard
St.
Bert's, 211 Renner Ave.
Dan's, 245 Academy St.
Little Johnny's, 47 Montgomery

Kesselman's, 13th & Rutgers St.
Alcazar, 72 Waverly Place
Rosen's, 164 Spruce St.
Dave's, 202 Court St.
Kleinbergs, 88 Waverly St.
Afro, 19 Quitman St.
Welcome Inn, 87 West St.
'570', 570 Market St.
Corprew's, 297 Springfield Ave.
Dug-Out, 188 Belmont Ave.
Harry's, 60 Waverly Ave.
Ernie's, 104 Wallace St.
Trippe's, 121 Halstead St.
Mulberry, 302 Mulberry St.
Frederick, 2 Boston St.
Hi Spot, 166 W. Kinney St.
Harold, 71 Bloomfield
Wood's, 258 Prince St.
NIGHT CLUBS
Piccadilly, 1 Peshine Ave.
Club Caravan, 3 Bedford St.
Hi Spot, 166 W. Kinney St.
New Kinney Club, 36 Arlington St.
Boston Plaza, 4 Boston St.
Golden Inn, 192 S. Pruce St.
Nest Club, Warren & Norfolk St.
Alcazar, 72 Waverly Ave.
Night Cap, 1079 Broad St.
CHINESE RESTAURANTS
Chinese-American, 603 W. Market
SERVICE STATIONS
Estes, 77 Tillinghast St.
GARAGES
Branch, 45 Rankin St.

OCEAN CITY

HOTELS
Comfort, 201 Bay Ave.
Washington, 6th & Simpson St.
Brydson's, 2878 6th & Simpson
Ave.
TOURIST HOMES
Edna Mae's, 921 West Ave.

ORANGE

HOTELS
Y.M.C.A., 84 Oakwood Ave.
Y.W.C.A., 66 Oakwood Ave.
RESTAURANTS
Triangle, 152 Barrow St.
Joe's, 120 Barrow St.
CHINESE RESTAURANTS
Orange Gardens, 122 Parrow St.
DRUG STORES
Central, Parrow & Hickory Sts.
TAILORS
Fitchitt, 99 Oakwood Ave.
Triangle, 101 Hickory St.

PAULSBORO

RESTAURANTS
Elsie's, 246 W. Adams St.

42

PATERSON
TAVERNS
Idle Hour Bar, 53 Bridge St.
Joymakers, 38 Bridge St.
GARAGES
Brown's, 57 Godwin St.

PERTH AMBOY
HOTELS
Lenora, 550 Hartford St.

POINT PLEASANT
TAVERNS
Joe's, 337 Railroad Ave.

PINE BROOK
TOURIST HOMES
RESTAURANTS

PLAINFIELD
TOURIST HOMES
Miss Daisy Robinson, 658 Essex St.
TAVERNS
Liberty, 4th St.

PLEASANTVILLE
TOURIST HOMES
Marionette Cot., 604 Portland Ave.
Virginia Inn, 1505 S. New Rd.
Garden Spot, 300 Doughty Rd.
TAVERNS
Harlem Inn, 1117 Washington Ave.
ROAD HOUSES
Martin's, 304 W. Wright St.

RED BANK
HOTELS
Robins Nest, 615 River Rd.
RESTAURANTS
Vincents, 263 Shrewsbury Ave.
TAVERNS
West Bergen, 103 W. Bergen Place
BARBER SHOPS
A. Dillard, 250 Shrewsbury Ave.
BEAUTY PARLORS
R. Alleyne, 124 W. Bergen Place
Suries, 261 Shrewsbury Ave.
SERVICE STATIONS
Galatres, Shrewsbury & Catherine
TAILORS
Dudley's, 79 Sunset Ave.

ROSELLE
TAVERNS
Omega, 302 E. 9th St.
St. George, 1139 St. George Ave.
RESTAURANTS
Hill Top, 60 Jerusalem Rd.
ROAD HOUSES
Villa Casanova, Jerusalem Rd.
COUNTRY CLUBS
Shady Rest, Jerusalem Rd.

SALEM
TAVERNS
Stith's, 111 Market St.

SEA BRIGHT
RESTAURANTS
Castle Inn, 11 New. St.

SEWAREN
TAILORS
Quality, 13 Pleasant Ave.

SHREWSBURY
SERVICE STATIONS
Rodney's, Shrewsbury Ave.

SUMMIT
HOTELS
Y.M.C.A., 393 Broad St.

TOMS RIVER
TAVERNS
Casaloma, Manitan Park

TRENTON
HOTELS
Y.M.C.A., 40 Fowler St.
RESTAURANTS
Spot Sandwich, 121 Spring St.
BEAUTY PARLORS
Bea's, 114 Spring St.
Geraldine's, 17 Trent St.
BARBER SHOPS
Sanitary, 199 N. Willow St.
Bill's, 105 Spring St.
NIGHT CLUBS
Famous, 228 N. Willow St.
ROAD HOUSES
Crossing Inn, Eggertt's Crossing

VAUX HALL
TAVERNS
Carnegie, 380 Carnegie Place

WILDWOOD
HOTELS
Pondexter Apts., 106 E. Schellinger Ave.
Glen Oak, 100 E. Lincoln St.
The Marion, Artic & Spicer Ave.
Artic Ave., 3600 Artic Ave.
V'esta, 4113 Park Blvd.
TOURIST HOMES
Dean's, 166 W. Young Ave.
Lilian's, 134 W. Baker Ave.
Mrs. E. Crawley, 3816 Artic
BEAUTY PARLORS
B. Johnson's, 407 Garfield Ave.
BARBER SHOPS
R. Morton, 4010 New Jersey Ave.
NIGHT CLUBS
High Steppers, 437 Lincoln Ave.

WOODBURY
RESTAURANTS
Robinson's, 225 Park Ave.

WEST PLEASANTVILLE
COUNTRY CLUB
Pine Acres Country Club

NEW YORK STATE

ALBANY
HOTELS
Hotel Broadway,
603 Broadway
Kenmore, 76 Columbia Ave.
TOURIST HOMES
Mrs. Aaron J. Oliver
42 Spring St.
RESTAURANTS
Dorsey's, Cor. Van Trumpet & B'way
BEAUTY PARLORS
Buelah Foods, 96 2nd St.
Westner, 643 Broadway
BARBER SHOPS
Martin's, 4 Vantromp St.
Westner, 643 Broadway
NIGHT CLUBS
Rythm Club, Madison Ave.
TAVERNS
King's, Cor. Green & Madison Sts.

ANGOLA
ROAD HOUSES
Leroy's Hacienda
Rt. No. 5, 20 miles west of Buffalo

BATH
TOURIST HOMES
Tuskegee, 364 West Morris St.

BUFFALO
HOTELS
Little Harlem, 494 Michigan Ave.
Y.M.M.C.A., 585 Michigan Ave.
Montgomery, 486 Michigan Ave.
Vendome, 177 Clinton St.
Claridge, 38 Broadway
TOURIST HOMES
Miss R. Scott, 244 N. Division St.
Mrs. F. Washington, 172 Clinton St.
Mrs. G. Chase, 194 Clinton St.
William Campbell, 342 Adam St.
RESTAURANTS
Horseshoe, 212 William St.
Crystal, 534 Broadway
Bar-B-Q, 413 Michigan Ave.
Empire, 454 Michigan Ave.
Elite, 280 Broadway
Apex, 311 William St.
Alfreda's, 192 Broadway
Peter Dubil, 535 Broadway
New China's, 172 Genesse St.
Panama, 378 Jefferson St.
CHINESE RESTAURANTS
Kam Wing Loo, 433 Michigan Ave.
BEAUTY PARLORS
Middleton, 229 Bond St.
Lady Esther's, 94 Florida St.
Orchid, 419 Pratt St.
Melisey's, 196 Hickory St.
La Ritz, 348 Jefferson Ave.

Matchless, 169 William St.
Edwards, 530 William St.
Jean's, 142 Adams St.
Laura's, 643 Broadway
La Mae, 437 Jefferson Ave.
Jessie's, 560 Spring St.
Fuqua's, 587 Clinton St.
Middleton, 384 Clinton St.
Bonita's, 254 William St.
BARBER SHOP
People's, 433 Williams St.
TAVERNS
Jay G. Stamper, Prop., 192 B'way
Pearls, 474 Michigan Ave.
Clover Leaf, 443 Michigan Ave.
TAVERNS
Apex, 311 Williams St.
Balser, 416 William St.
Kern's, 382 William St.
Hickory, Hickory & Williams
Horse Shoe, Williams & Pine
Toussaint, 292 Williams St.
Joe's, 416 William St.
Glass Horseshoe, 214 Williams St.
Jamboree, 339 Williams St.
Mandy's, 278 Williams St.
Polly's, 483 Jefferson St.
Dubil's, 535 Broadway
Zarin, 557 Clinton St.
Parkside, 452 William St.
NIGHT CLUBS
Moonglow, Michigan & Williams
Horseshoe, William & Pine Sts.
LIQUOR STORES
Swan, Swan & Hickory St.
Aqui-Line, 141 Broadway
Ferry, 192 E. Ferry St.
Stenson's, 133 William St.
SERVICE STATIONS
Fraas, Clinton & Jefferson
Your Tire, 250 Broadway
TAILORS
Eagle, 414 Eagle St.
Reeve's, 119 Clinton St.
Mickey's, 544 Williams St.
Sam's, 270 William St.
Byrd's, 473 Broadway
Bell, 197 William St.
Sam's, 270 William St.
Empire's Star, 234 Broadway
TAXI CABS
Veterans, 120 William St.
DRUG STORES
Wilmar's, 432 William St.
Roebrts, 467 William St.

ELMIRA
TOURIST HOMES
Green Pastures, 670 Dickinson St.

ITHACA
NIGHT CLUBS
Elk's, 119 So. Tioga St.
Forest City, 119 So. Tioga St.

GLENN FALLS
TOURIST HOMES
Hayes Cottage, 99 Sanford St.
Mrs. M. Mayberry, 16 Ferry St.

HUGUENOT
TOURIST HOMES
Janeal Lodge, P. O. Box 23

JAMESTOWN
TOURIST HOMES
Mrs. I. W. Herald, 51 W. 10th St
Mrs. J. M. Brown, 198 W. 11th St

KINGSTON
HOTELS
Gordon, 3 Canal St.

MECHANICVILLE
TOURIST HOMES
Green's, R.F.D. No. 1

NIAGARA FALLS
TOURIST HOMES
The Hutchinson's
1050 Center Ave.
TOURIST PLACEMENT for GROUPS
W. L. Parker, 627 Erie Ave.
Mack Hayes House, 437 1 St.
Mrs. Ralph W. Reynolds
419 1st St.
Mrs. Alice Ford, 413 First St.
Mrs. Brown, 1202 Haeberle Ave.
Mr. & Mrs. T. R. Davis
319 12th St.
A. E. Gabriel, 635 Erie Ave.
Mrs. M. Francis, 219 10th St.
Mrs. F. T. Young, 421 1st St.
TAVERNS
Cephas, 621 Erie Ave.

NYACK
NIGHT CLUBS
Paradise, Cedar Hill Ave.

PORT JERVIS
TOURIST HOMES
R. Pendelton, 26 Bruce St.

POUGHKEEPSIE
TOURIST HOMES
Mrs. S. Osterholt, 16 Crannell St.

ROCHESTER
HOTELS
Gibson, 461 Clariss St.
TOURIST HOMES
Mrs. Allie O. King, 456 Clarissa St.
Mrs. Latimer, 176 Clarissa St.
RESTAURANTS
La Rue, 491 Clarissa St.
Chicken Shack, 371 Clarissa St.
BEAUTY PARLORS
Beauty Salon, 481 Clarissa St.
Hawkins, 36 Favor St.

BARBER SHOPS
Blackstone's, 399 Clarissa St.
Hawkins, 36 Favor St.
TAILORS
Bright Star, 367 Clarissa St.
Walker's, 149 Adams St.
TAVERNS
Dawn, 314 Clarissa St.
Vallot's, 439 Clarissa St.
Rollin's, 118 Joseph Ave.
Cotton Club, 222 Joseph Ave.
Dan's, 293 Clarissa St.
LIQUOR STORES
Kaplan's, 346 Clarissa St.
GARAGES
Clarissa St., Cor. Spring & Clarissa Sts.
Derham's, 40 Cypress St.
SERVICE STATIONS
A & A, Cor. Beaver & Clarissa

SCHENECTADY
TOURIST HOME
Mrs. Grant Thomas, 1024 Albany
HOTELS
Foster House, 310 Dakota St.
BEAUTY PARLORS
Nixons, 558 Broadway
La Belle Femme, 806 Hamilton St.
Elizabeths, 545 Liberty St.
BARBER SHOPS
Russell's, 351 Broadway
Lee Washington, 530 Liberty St.
TAVERNS
Eljor, 348 Broadway
TAXI CABS
Billy, 348 Broadway

SARATOGA SPRINGS
RESTAURANTS
Spuyten Duyvil, 157 George St.
TOURIST HOMES
LaFleur, 21 Cowan St.
James, 17 Park St.
Mrs. John Parker, 18 Cherry St.

SYRACUSE
BEAUTY PARLORS
Tifferroa's, 422 Harrison St.
BARBER SHOPS
New York, 612 So. Townsend St.
HOTELS
The Savoy, 518 E. Washington St.
TOURIST HOMES
The Sylvan, 815 E. Fayette St.
Y.M.C.A., 340 Montgomery St.
W. R. Farrish, 809 E. Fayette St.
RESTAURANTS
Aunt Edith's, 601½ Harrison St.
TAVERNS
Coles, 825 Townsend St.
Penguin, 822 S. State St.
Copacabana, 725 S. Townsend St.
BEAUTY PARLORS
Tifferroa's, 313 S. McBride St
Webb's, 512 Almond St.

45

BARBER SHOPS
Smith's, 600½ E. Washington St.
New York, 62 So. Townsend St.
John Dove's, 529 Harrison St.
Smith's, 600½ E. Washington St.
NIGHT CLUBS
Goldie's, 423 Harrison St.
LIQUOR STORES
MulRoy's, 361 E. Genessee St.
Ben's, 601 Harrison St.
La Rock's, 442 E. Jefferson St.
DRUG STORES
A & B, 724 S. McBride St.
Singer's, 833 E. Genessee St.
Thornton's, 900 E. Fayette St.
Horton's, 615 Almond St.
TAILORS
Jackson's, 904 E. Fayette St.
Bennie's, 512 Harrison St.

UTICA

TOURIST HOMES
Broad St. Inn, 415 Broad St.
Howard Home, 413 Broad St.

WATERTOWN

HOTELS
Woodruff, Public Square
TOURIST HOMES
E. F. Thomas, 123 Union St.
V. H. Brown, 502 Binase St.
G .E. Deputy, 711 Morrison St.
Mrs. Ruth Thomas, 556 Morrison St.
RESTAURANTS
Capitol, Court Square
BARBER SHOPS
Chicago, Court St.
BEAUTY PARLORS
Mrs. Nancy Williams, 436 Edmonds
SERVICE STATIONS
Reilly Esso Station, 496 Edmonds
GARAGES
Guilfoyle, Stone St.

WESTBROOKVILLE

TOURIST HOME
White Horse Lodge

NEW YORK, N.Y.

(HARLEM)

HOTELS
Braddock, 126th & 8th Ave.
El Melrah, 19 W. 135th St.
Woodside, 2424 7th Ave.
Grampion, 182 St. Nicholas Ave.
Y.M.C.A., 180 W. 135th St.
Y.W.C.A., 175 W. 137th St.

Hotel Revella
307 West 116th St.
Phone: UNiversity 4-9825
Elton, 227 W. 135th St.
Cadillac, 235 W. 135th St.
Rich's Plaza, 35 Bradhurst Ave.
Mel's Plaza, 151 W. 118th St.
America, 145 West 47th St.
Garret Hotel, 314 W. 127th St.
Crosstown, 515 W. 145th St.

Richard Hotel,
6 Bradhurst Ave.
Harriet Hotels, 313 W. 127th St.
Cambridge, 141 W. 110th St.
Martha, 6 W. 135th St.
Welthon, 2057 7th Ave.
Dewey Square, 201-203 W. 117th St.
The Tenrub, 328 St. Nicholas
Beakford, 300 W. 116th St.

Hotel Theresa,
2090 7th Ave.
Mariette, 176 W. 121st St.
Currie, 101 W. 145th St.
Cecil, 208 W. 118th St.
Revella, 307 W. 116th St.
Hudson, 1649 Amsterdam Ave.
Barbera, 501 W. 142nd St.

Crosstown Hotel
515 West 145th St.
Hotel Elmeneh, 845 St. Nicholas
Douglas, 809 St. Nicholas Ave.
Manhattan, 504 Manhattan Ave.
Delta, 409 W. 145th St.
Edgecombe, 345 Edgecombe
Crosstown, 515 W. 145th St.
Parkview, 55 W. 110th St.
RESTAURANTS
Pete's, 2534 7th Ave.
Surprise, 2319 7th Ave.
Lulu Belle's, 317 W. 126th St.
Four Star, 2433 7th Ave.

for...
for Sightseeing
in New York

By Bus   By Boat

Special Rates for Groups of
25 or More

No Service Charge

Write or Contact

VICTOR H. GREEN & COMPANY

200 West 135th Street   Room 215A   New York 30, N. Y.

Esquire Lunchonette, 2201 7th Ave.
Brown's, 210 W. 135th St.
E & M, 2016 7th Ave.
Em & Bee, 458 Lenox Ave.
Davis', 2066 7th Ave.
Pals Inn, 307 W. 125th St.
Little Shack, 2267 7th Ave.
Jimmy's, 763 St. Nicholas Ave.
Rose Meta, 9 W. 125th St.
The Lotus, 451 Lenox Ave.
Jennie Lou's, 2297 7th Ave.
Hamburg Paradise, 377 W. 125th St.
Jimmie's, 307 W. 125th St.
Beverly Hills, 303 W. 145th St.
Frazier's, 2067 7th Ave.
Shalimar, 2065 7th Ave.

TOURIST HOMES
Mrs. Agnes Babb, 68 E. 127th St.

CHINESE RESTAURANTS
Mayling, 1723 Amsterdam Ave.

BEAUTY PARLORS
Frankie's, 2380 7th Ave.
Elite, 2544 7th Ave.
Myers & Griffin, 65 W. 134th St.
National, 301 W. 144th St.
Neuway, 143 W. 116th St.
Beard's, 322 St. Nicholas Ave.
Bonnie's, 165 W. 127th St.
Mme. Ruth's, 259 W. 116th St.

BARBER SHOPS
Sportsman, 268½ W. 135th St.
Davis, 69 W. 138th St.
Renaissance, 2349 7th Ave.
Delux, 92 St. Nicholas Pl.
World, 2621 8th Ave.

Dunbar, 2808 8th Ave.
Hi-Hat, 2276 7th Ave.
Ideal, 716 St. Nicholas Ave.
Modernistic, 2132 7th Ave.
Service, 2296 7th Ave.
Blue Castle, 1361 Amsterdam Ave.
Early Dawn, 2570 7th Ave.
The Esquire, 2265 7th Ave.
Tuxedo, 1925 Amsterdam Ave.

TAVERNS
El Favorito Bar, 2055 8th Ave.
International, 2150 5th Ave.
Arhtur's, 2481 8th Ave.
Red Tip, 2470 7th Ave.
John Allen's, 207 W. 116th St.
Brittwood, 594 Lenox Ave.
Frankie's Cafe, 2328 7th Ave.
Bank's, 2338 8th Ave.
Brownie's, 2571 7th Ave.
Bogan's, 2154 8th Ave.
Frank Lezama, 3578 Broadway
Palm, 209 W. 125th St.
Frank's, 313 W. 125th St.
William's, 2011 7th Ave.
Harris' Corner, 132nd St. & 7th Ace.
Dawn, 1931 Amsterdam Ave.
Pasadena, 2350 8th Ave.
Jack Carters, 1590 7th Ave.
Poor John's, 2268 8th Ave.
Farrell's, 2175 7th Ave.
Chico's, 2014 Fifth Ave.
Braddock, Cor. 126th St. & 8th Ave.
Jock's, 2350 7th Ave.
Tom Farrell's, 128th St. & Convent Ave.

47

George's, 630 Lenox Ave.
Sugar Ray's, 2074 7th Ave.
Hawkin's, 308 W. 125th St.
Apollo, 303 W. 125th St.
Baby Grand, 319 W. 125th St.
Al's, 415 W. 125th St.
Horseshoe, 2474 7th Ave.
Lou's, 1985 Amsterdam Ave.
Welcome Inn, 2895 8th Ave.
Tom Delaney, 7th Ave. & 137th St.
Blue Heaven, 378 Lenox Ave.
Colonial, 116 Bradhurst Ave.
Eddie's, 714 St. Nicholas Ave.
Hot-Cha, 2280 7th Ave.
La Mar Cheri, 739 St. Nicholas Ave.
Logas, 2496 7th Ave.
Monte Carlo, 2347 7th Ave.
Murrain, 635 Lenox Ave.
Victoria, 2418 7th Ave.
Fat Man, St. Nicholas Ave. & 155th
Jimmie Daniels, 114 W. 116th St.
Moon Glow, 2461 7th Ave.
George Farrell's, 2711 8th Ave.
Novelty Bar & Grill, 1965 Amsterdam Ave.
L-Bar, 3601 Broadway
Chick's Bar & Grill, 2501 7th Ave.
Sport's Inn, 2308 8th Ave.
Clover Bar & Grill, 1735 Amsterdam Ave.
Daniel's, 2461 7th Ave.
Coran's, 2359 7th Ave.
Pelican, 45 Lenox Ave.
Mandalay, 2201 7th Ave.
Dawn Cafe, 1931 Amsterdam Ave.
Chateau Lounge, 379 W. 125th St.
Well's, Musical Bar, 2249 7th Ave.
Firpo's, 503 Lenox Ave.
Zambezi, 2267 7th Ave.
Mardi Gras, 1951 Amsterdam Ave.
Casbah, 163rd St. & St. Nicholas
Bowman's, 92 St. Nicholas Pl.
Renny, 2359 7th Ave.
Elk Scene, 439 Lenox Ave.
Magnet, 570 Lenox Ave.
Fez, 1955 7th Ave.
Frankie's, 2328 7th Ave.
Bird Cage, 2308 7th Ave .
Bali, 2096 Amsterdam Ave.

NIGHT CLUBS

Savannah Club, "66" 68 W. 3rd St.
Reno, 549 W. 145th St.
Elk's Rendezvous, 133rd & Lenox
Celebrity Club, 35 E. 125th St.
Murrain's, 132nd & 7 Ave.
Hollywood Club, 116th & Lenox
Lenox Rendezvous, 75 Lenox Ave.
Harlem, 266 W. 145th St.
Lido, 35 W. 125th St.
Club Harlem, 266 W. 145th St.
Gold Coast Lounge, 2617 5th Ave.
Well's Musical Bar, 2249 7th Ave.
Bowman's, 92 St. Nicholas Pl.
Paradise, 8th Ave. at 110th St.

LIQUOR STORES

Convent, 42 Convent Ave.
Charity, 483 W. 150 St.
Daniel Burrows, 760 St. Nicholas
Eulace Peacock, 200 W. 140th St.
Ferguson, 271 W. 126th St.
Fitton & Telesford, 300½ W. 116th
Green's, 161 W. 120th St.
H. & S., 5 W. 131st St.
Harlem, 85 W. 128th St.
Inez Gumbs, 347 W. 120th St.
C. D. Kings, 2087 Madison Ave.
Padam's, 1963 Amsterdam Ave.
Chas. Arshen, 2501 8th Ave.
Forbes, 272 W. 154th St.
Hamilton Place, 150 Hamilton Pl.
H & R, 273 W. 121st St.
Roy Campanella, 7th Ave. & 134 St.
Goldman's, 483 W. 155th St.

DRUG STORES

M. Boutte, 1928 St. Nicholas Ave.

GARAGES

Colonial Park, 310 W. 144th St.
Polo Grounds, 155th St. & St. Nicholas Ave.
Dumas, 226 W. 135th St.
Park Lane, 1890 Park Ave.

TAILORS

Robert Lewis, 1980 7th Ave.
Globe, 2594 8th Ave.
7th Ave., 2051 7th Ave.
Little Alpha, 200 W. 136th St.
Dig-By, 300 W. 111th St.
La Fontaine, 470 Convent Ave.
Hill Side, 513 W. 145th St.
Dillette's, 101 ..dgecombe Ave.

SERVICE STATIONS

Park Lane, 1890 Park Ave.

DANCE HALLS

Savoy, Lenox Ave. & 140th St.
Golden Gate, Lenox Ave. & 142th

BROOKLYN

HOTELS

GARFIELD HOTEL

Newly Furnished and Decorated

160 REID AVE., BROOKLYN, N. Y.

Bet. Gates Ave. & Monroe St.

Tel.: GLenmore 5-1094

Pleasant Manor, 218 Gates Ave.
Garfield, 160 Reid Ave.
Lincoln Terrace, 1483 Pacific St.
Y.M.C.A., 405 Carlton Ave.
Burma, 145 Gates Ave.
Lefferts, 127 Lefferts Place
Garfield, 160 Reid Ave.

RESTAURANTS

Commodore, 486 Thompkins Ave.
Continental, 706 Nostrand Ave.
Jackson's, 1558 Fulton St.

Dew Drop, 363 Halsey St.
Little Roxy, 490A Summer Ave.
Bernice's Cafeteria, 105 Kingston Ave.
Spick & Span, 70 Kingston Ave.
G & H, 382 Summers Ave.
Caravan, 377 Hancock St.

CHINESE RESTAURANTS
Chung King, 1139 Fulton St.
New Shanghai, 361 Nostrand Ave.
Fulton Palace, 1139 Fulton St.

BEAUTY PARLORS
Berlena's, 186 Jefferson
Bartley's, 1125 Fulton St.
Katherine's, 345 Sumner Ave.
Ideal, 285A Sumner Ave.
Mariett's, 451 Nostrand Ave.
Edith's, 389 Tompkins Ave.
LaRoberts, 322 Macon St.

BEAUTY CULTURE SCHOOLS
Theresa, 304 Livonia Ave.

TAVERNS
Riviera, Bedford & Brevoort Pl.
Brownie's, 714 St. Marks Pl.
Flamingo, 259 A Kingston Ave.
Topside, 537 Marcy Ave.
Palm Gardens, 491 Summer Ave.
Royal, 1073 Fulton St.
Parkside, 759 Gates Ave.
Decatur Bar & Grill,, 301 Reid Ave.
Kingston Tavern, 1496 Fulton St.
Arlington Inn, 1253 Fulton St.
Disler's, 759 Gates Ave.
Veorna Leafe, 1330 Fulton St.
K & C Tavern, 588 Gates Ave.
Smitty's, 286 Patchen Ave.
Casablanca, 300 Reid Ave.
Country Cottage, 375 Franklin Ave.
Bombay, 377 Christopher St.
Capitol, 1550 Fulton St.
Traveler's, Inn, 5A Hull St.
Marion's, 125 Marion St.
Ward's, 480 Halsey St.
Tip Top, 1750 Fulton St.
Topside, 537 Marcy Ave.
Berry Bros., 1714 Fulton St.
Logan's, 1165 Bradford Ave.
Bar 688, 688 Halsey St.
Brooklyn Fraternal, 1068 Fulton St.
Jefferson, 397 Tompkins Ave.
Bushwick, 375 Bushwick Ave.
Lorene's, 373 Nostrand Ave.
Turbo Village, 249 Reid Ave.
Elmo, 243 Reid Ave.
Summer, 693 Gates Ave.
New Durkin, 1285 Fulton St.
Esquire, Atlantic & Kingston Aves.
Frank's Caravan, 377 Hancock St.
Hollywood, Cor. Gates & Nostrand Aves.
Cross Roads, Cor. Bedford & Fulton Sts.
Laredo Bar, 1624 Fulton St.

NIGHT CLUBS
Ebony, 1330 Fulton St.
Baby Grand, 1274 Fulton St.

DRUG STORES
Provident, 1265 Bedford Ave.
Bancroft, Franklin & Bergen St.

WINE & LIQUOR STORES
Yak, 1361 Fulton St.
Lincoln, 401 Tompkins Ave.
York, 1361 Fulton St.
Stuyvesant, 1551 Fulton St.
Allen Rose, 106 Kingston Ave.
Turner's, 249 Sumner St.
Gottesman's, 41 Albany Ave.
Sexton's, 616 Halsey St.

TAILORS
Bea Jay, 1722 Fulton St.

BRONX

HOTELS
Guest House, 744 Kelly St.
Carver, 980 Prospect Ave.
Crotona, 695 E. 170th St.

RESTAURANTS
Daniel's, 1107 Prospect Ave.

BEAUTY PARLORS
Grayson, 874 Prospect Ave.
Glennada, 875 Longwood Ave.

BARBER SHOPS
Modern, 1174 Boston Rd.

TAVERNS
Freddie's Bar, 1204 Boston Rd.
Harty's Mid-Way, 458 E. 165th St.
Neighborhood, 3344 Third Ave.
Louis' Tavern, 3510 Third Ave.
Kennie's, 853 Freeman St.
Lucille's, 3800 Third Ave.
Jimmy's, 267 E. 161st St.
Zombie Bar, 1745 Boston Rd.
Rainbow Gardens, 977 Prospect Ave.
B & P, 823 E. 169th St.
Trinity, 163rd & Trinity Ave.
Ralph Rida's, 1155 Tinton Ave.
Crystal Lounge, 1035 Prospect Ave.
Five Corners, 169th St. & Boston Rd
Sporting Life, 950 Prospect Ave.
Central, 267 E. 161st St.
DeLuxe, 270 E. 161st St.
Alamo, 1056 Boston Rd.

WINE AND LIQUOR STORES
Franklin Ave., 1214 Franklin Ave.
Prospect, 889 Prospect Ave.
West Farms, 2026 Boston Rd.
O'Connell's, 1311 Boston Rd.

NIGHT CLUBS
845-845 Prospect Ave.

BALLROOM
McKinley, 1258 Boston Rd.

SERVICE STATIONS
Al & Jim's, Boston Rd. & 170th St.

LONG ISLAND

AMITYVILLE

RESTAURANTS
Watervliet, 158 Dixon Ave.
ROAD HOUSES
Freddy's, Albany & Banbury Court
BARBER SHOPS
Jimmy's, Albany & Brewster
BEAUTY PARLORS
Boyd's, 21 Banbury Court

CORONA

TAVERNS
Big George, 106 Northern Blvd.
Prosperity, 32-19 103rd St.
NIGHT CLUBS
New Cameo, 108 Northern Blvd.
BEAUTY PARLORS
Myrt's, 105-09 Northern Blvd.
RESTAURANTS
Encore, 105-13 Northern Blvd.

FREEPORT

NIGHT CLUBS
Celebrity, 77 E. Sunrise H'way

HEMPSTEAD

TAVERNS
BARBER SHOPS
Modernistic, 96 So. Franklin St.
BEAUTY PARLORS
Sykes, 98 So. Franklin St.

INWOOD

NIGHT CLUBS
Club Carib, 333 Bayview Ave.

JAMAICA

TAVERNS
Palm Gardens, 107-02 Merrick
Tolliver's, 112-27 New York Blvd.
Mandalay, 114-16 Merrick Rd.
Hank's, 108-04 New York Blvd.
Old Sweet, 158-11 South Rd.
TAILORS
Klugh's, 107-21 171st St.
BEAUTY PARLORS
Roslyn, 106-53 New York Blvd.

LINDENHURST

NIGHT CLUBS
Club Ebony, Sunrise H'way 40th St.

SPRINGFIELD

BEAUTY PARLORS
Gorja, 126-17 Merrick Blvd.

ST. ALBANS

LIQUOR STORE
Frank Maybrs, 119-06 Merrick Blvd
NIGHT CLUBS
Ruby, 175-02 Baisley Blvd.

STATEN ISLAND

WEST BRIGHTON

BEAUTY PARLORS
Etta's, 1652 Richmond Terr.
BARBER SHOPS
Dozier, 192 Broadway
NIGHT CLUBS
Williams, 208 Broadway
TAILORS
A. Higgs, 721 Henderson
Tucker, 260 Broadway
SERVICE STATIONS
Rispoli, 46 Barker St.

WESTCHESTER

ELMSFORD
TAVERNS
Clarke, 91 Saw Mill River Rd.

MT. VERNON
TOURIST HOME
Mrs. Lloyd King, 343 So. 10th Ave.
RESTAURANTS
Hamburger, 15 W. 3 St.
Friendship, 50 W. 3rd St.
TAVERNS
Mohawk Inn, 142 S. 7th Ave.
Friendship Center, 50 W. 3rd St.

NEW ROCHELLE
HOTELS
Huguenot, 242 Huguenot St.
RESTAURANTS
Harris, 29 Morris St.
Week's, 68 Winyah Ave.
BEAUTY PARLORS
A. Berry, 50 DeWitts Pl.
B. Miller, 54 DeWitts Pl.
Ocie, 41 Rochelle Pl.
BARBER SHOPS
Field's, 66 Winyah Ave.
Bal-Mo-Ral, 56 Brook St.
LIQUOR STORES
A. Edwards, 112 Union Ave.
DRUG STORES
Daniel's, 57 Lincoln Ave.

NORTH TARRYTOWN
BARBER SHOPS
Lemon's, Valley St.

TUCKAHOE
RESTAURANTS
Butterfly Inn, 47 Washington St.
BEAUTY PARLORS
Shanhana, 144 Main St.
BARBER SHOPS
Al's, 144 Main St.

YONKERS
RESTAURANTS
The Brown Derby, 125 Nepperham Ave.

WHITE PLAINS
HOTELS
Rel Rio, 122 Lafayette Ave.
RESTAURANTS
Walnard's, 79 Martine Ave.
Waldorf, 102 Grove St.
Tarks, 372 Central Ave.
Field's, 338 Tarrytown Rd.
BEAUTY PARLORS
Reynold's, 144 Main St.
Maudie's, 123 Martine Ave.
BARBER SHOPS
Mitchell's, 100 Grove St.
NIGHT CLUBS
Shelton's, 53 Grove St.

LIQUOR STORES
Martine, 120 Martine Ave.
TAVERNS
Field's, 538 Tarrytown Rd.
Sonny's, 397 Tarrytown Rd.
TAXI CABS
Martine, 85 Martine Ave.
Bower, 106 Grove St.
TAILORS
Johnson's, 121 Martine Ave.

NEVADA
RENO
TOURIST HOMES

HAWTHORNE GUEST
Catering to Tourists - Phone 3-7386
OPEN YEAR ROUND
Rec. by Chamber of Commerce,
also A.A.A.
J. R. HAMLET, Prop.
542 Valley Road   Reno, Nevada

Floyd Garner, 857 E. 2nd St.
LAS VEGAS
TOURIST HOMES
Harrison's Guest House
1001 North 8 'F' St.
Shaw Apts., 619 Van Buren St.

NEW HAMPSHIRE
WHITEFIELD
TOURIST HOMES
Mrs. Homer Mason, Greenwood St.

NEW MEXICO
ALBUQUERQUE
TOURIST HOMES
Mrs. Kate Duncan, 423 N. Arno St.
Mrs. W. Bailey, 1127 N. 2nd St.
RESTAURANTS
Aunt Brenda's, 406 North Arno St.
CARLSBAD
TOURIST HOMES
Mrs. A. Sherrell, 502 S. Haloquens
BARBER SHOPS
Garland Johnson, West Bronson St.
GALLUP
TOURIST HOMES
Mrs. Sonnie Lewis, 109 Wilson St.
ROSWELL
TOURIST HOMES
Mrs. Mary Collins
121 East 10th St.
R. Brown, 313 W. Math
RESTAURANTS
Sun Set Cafe, 115 E. Walnut St

51

TUCUMCARI
TOURIST HOMES
Rockett Inn
524 W. Campbell St.
Jone's Rooms, Box 1002
J. E. Mitchell, 406 N. 3rd S.
Mitchell's Rooms
406 North 3rd St.
GARAGES
Swift's, Hi'way 66

NORTH CAROLINA

ASHEVILLE
HOTELS
James Keys, 409 Southside Ave.
Y.W.C.A., 360 College St.
Booker T. Washington, 409 Southside
TOURIST HOMES
Savoy, Eagle & Market Sts.
RESTAURANTS
Palace Grille, 19 Eagle St.
BARBER SHOPS
Wilson's, 13 Eagle St.
Jamison, 211 Ashland Ave.

BLADENBORO
BEAUTY PARLORS
Lacy's Beauty Shop

CHARLOTTE
HOTELS
Alexander, 523 N. McDowell St.
RESTAURANTS
Ingram's, 304 So. McDowell St.
BEAUTY PARLORS
Martha's, 509 E. 2nd St.
BARBER SHOPS
2nd St., 500 E. 2nd St.
Martha's, 508 E. 2nd St.
DRUG STORES
Charlotte, 200 E. Trade St.
Carolina, 401 E. Trade St.
TAILORS
New Way, 935 E. 9th St.
SERVICE STATIONS
Bishop Dale, 1st & Brevard Sts.
Bob Roberson's, 701 Trade St.

DURHAM
HOTELS
Biltmore, 332½ E. Pettigrew St.
Jones, 502 Ramsey St.
RESTAURANTS
Elivira's, 801 Fayetteville St.
Bull City, 412 Pettigrew
Cu-Cu, 916 Pickets
College Inn, 1306 Fayetteville

BEAUTY PARLORS
De Shazors, 809 Fayetteville St.
D'Orsay, 120 S. Mangum St.
Friendly City, 711 Fayetteville St.
Burma's, 536 E. Pettigrew St.
Vanity Fair, 1508 Fayetteville St.
BARBER SHOPS
Friendly, 711 Fayetteville St.
TAVERNS
Hollywood, 118 S. Mangum St.
College Inn, 1306 Fayetteville St.
Jack's Grill, 706 Fayettev ille St.
SERVICE STATIONS
Granite, Main & 9th St.
Pine Ctreet, 1102 Pine St.
Williams, Cor. Pettigrew & Pine Sts.
Biltmore, 402 E. Pettigrew St.
Clay's, 406 1-2 Pettigrew St.
Speight's, Fayetteville & Pettigrew
Sulton's Esso, 400 Pine St.
DRUG STORES
Garrett's Biltmore, E. Pettigrew St.
Bull City, 610 Fayetteville St.
TAILORS
Royal Cleaners
538 E. Pettigrew St.
Boykin, 715 Fayetteville St.
Service, 612 Fayetteville St.
Union, 418 Dowd St.
Scott & Roberts, 702 Fayetteville

ELIZABETH CITY
TAVERNS
Blue Duck Inn, 404½ Ehringhaus
SERVICE STATIONS
Small's, Cor. S. Rd. & Roanoke Ave.

ELIZABETHTOWN
BEAUTY PARLORS
Liola's Beauty Salon
TAVERNS
Gill's Grill
Royal Cafe
DRUG STORES
McKay & Neal

ENFIELD
RESTAURANTS
Royal, 301 Highway St.

FAYETTEVILLE
HOTELS
Restful Inn, 418 Gillespie St.
TOURIST HOMES
Jones' Tourist Home
311 Moore St.
Mrs. L. C. McNeil, 418 Gillespie St.
RESTAURANTS
Mayflower Grill, N. Hillsboro St.
Silver Grill, 115 Gillespie St.
Arthur's Seafood rGill, 637 Person
"Vpoint", Murchison Rd.
Silver Girll, 115 Gillespie St.

BEAUTY PARLORS
  Brown's, 133 Person St.
  Royal Beauty Parlor, 127½ Person
  Modiste, 130½ Person St.
  Ethel's, Gillespie St.
BARBER SHOPS
  DeLux, Pesno St.
  Mack's, 117 Gillespie St.
TAVERNS
  Jack's, 213 Hillsboro St.
SERVICE STATIONS
  Moore's, 613 Ramsey St.
GARAGES
  Jeffrie's, Blount St.
TAILORS
  Gregory's, 1219 Ft. Bragg Rd.

GOLDSBORO
DRUG STORES
  Jackson's, So. James St.
TAILORS
  Garris, 208 N. Center St.
RESTAURANTS
  Scott's, 404 Gully St.
SHAVING PARLORS
  Thornton's, Teenage, 507 Alvin St.
BEAUTY PARLORS
  Raynard's, 619 Devereaux St.

GREENSBORO
HOTELS
  Plaza Manor, 511 Martin St.
  Legion Club, 829 E. Market St.
TOURIST HOMES
  T. Daniels, 912 E. Market St.
  Mrs. Lewis, 829 E. Market St.
  I. W. Wooten, 41 Lindsay St.
TAVERNS
  Paramount, 907 E. Market St.
TAILORS
  Shoffners, 922 E. Market St.
TAXI CABS
  MacRae, 106 S. Macon St.

GREENVILLE
RESTAURANTS
  Paradise, 314 Albermale Ave.
  Bell's, 310 Albermarle Ave.
BEAUTY SHOPS
  Spain, 614 Atlantic Ave.
DRUG STORES
  Harrison's, 908 Dickerson St.

HALLSBORO
BEAUTY PARLORS
  Leigh's, Route No. 1

HAMLET
CABINS
  C. B. Covington, North Yard

HENDERSON
TOURIST HOMES
Adams Tourist Home
526 Chestnut St.
TAXI CABS
  Green & Chavis, 720 Eaton St.

HIGH POINT
HOTELS
  Kilby's, 627½ E. Washington St.
KINGS MOUNTAIN
TOURIST HOMES
  Mrs. L. E. Ricks
KINGSTON
SERVICE STATIONS
  Daves, 205 E. South St.
LITTLETON
HOTELS
  Young's Hotel
LUMBERTON
HOTEL
  Spring's Inn, 103 Chestnut St.
LEXINGTON
SERVICE STATIONS
  D. T. Taylor, Esso Service
MT. OLIVE
RESTAURANTS
  Black Beauty Tea Room
NEW BERN
HOTELS
  Rhone, 42 Queen St.
TOURIST HOMES
  H. C. Sparrow, 65 West St.
RALEIGH
DRIVE IN RESTAURANTS
  Nile-Congo, Rt. 70 & Garner Rd.
  2½ Miles East
HOTELS
De Luxe Hotel
220 E. Cabarrus St.
  Arcade, 122 E. Hargett St.
  Y.M.C.A., 600 So. Bloodworth St.
  Lewis Hotel, 200 Cabarrus St.
TOURIST HOMES
Starksville Guest House
809 E. Bragg St.
  Mrs. Charles Higgs, 219 E. Lenoir
  Mrs. Pattie Higgs, 313 N. Tarboro
RESTAURANTS
  Owens, 125 E. Hargett St.
  New York, 108 E. Hargett St.
  Stanton's, Cafe, 319 South East St.
TAVERNS
  Tip Toe Inn, Cor. Davis & Blood-
    worth Sts.
BEAUTY PARLORS
  Hall's, 222 N. Tarboro St.
  Sales, 222 S. Tarboro St.
TAILORS
  G. & M., 106 Hargett St.
  Lewis, 220 E. Cabarrus St.
  Arcade ,122 E. Hargett St.
  Peerless, 516 Fayetteville St.
  Snakenburg, 123 So. Salisbury St.

GARAGES
Richradson & Smith, 108 E. Lenoir St.
TAXI CABS
East End, Dial 2-2086
PINEHURST
TOURIST HOMES
Foster's
SERVICE STATIONS
Foster's
ROCKY MOUNT
RESTAURANTS
Dixie, 106 E. Thomas
SERVICE STATIONS
Atlantic, 216 E. Thomas St.
Shaws, 440 Raleigh Rd.
SALISBURY
TAXI CABS
Safety, 122 N. Lee St.
SANFORD
DRUG STORES
Bland's, 300 S. Steele St.
SUMTER
TAVERNS
Silver Moon, 20 W. Liberty St.
WELDON
HOTELS
Pope
Terminal Inn, Washington Ave.
WHITEVILLE
TOURIST HOMES
Mrs. Fannie Jeffers, Mill St.
WILSON
HOTELS
The Wilson Biltmore, 539 E. Nash
TAXI CABS
M. Jones, 1209 E. Queen St.
WINSTON SALEM
HOTELS
Belmont, 601½ No. Patterson St.
Lincoln, 9 E. 3rd St.
Y.M.C.A., 410 N. Church St.
TOURIST HOMES
Charles H. Jones, 1611 E. 14th St.
Mrs. H. L. Christian, 302 E. 9th St.
WILMINGTON
HOTELS
Murphy, 813 Castle St.
TOURIST HOMES
Charles F. Payne
417 North 6th St.
RESTAURANTS
Johnson's, 1007 Chestnut St.
Ollie's, 415½ S. 7th St.
Blue Bird, 618 Castle St.
BEAUTY PARLORS
Beth's, 416 Anderson St.
Lezora, 609 Red Cross St.
Germany's, 715 Red Cross St.
Lou's, 820 Red Cross St.
Newkirk's, 1217 Castle St.

Pierce's, 615 Kedder St.
Apex, 613 Red Cross St.
Dickson, 1161 S. 7th St.
Gertrude, 415 S. 7th St.
Howard's, 121 S. 13th St.
Vanity Box, 115 S. 13th St.
La May, 703 S. 15th St.
Thelma's, 207 S. 12th St.
Zan-Zibar, 403 Nixon St.
McCleese, 9th & Red Cross Sts.
BARBER SHOPS
Johnson's, 6 Market St.
Brown's, 607 S. 7th St.
NIGHT CLUBS
TAVERNS
William's, 8th & Dawson Sts.
SERVICE STATIONS
Brooklyn, 4th & Taylor Sts
GARAGES
Fennell's, 124 So. 13th St.
DRUG STORES
Lane's, 4th & Bladen Sts.
TAXI CABS
Star, Dial 9259
Mack's, Dial 7645
Dixie, 516 S. 7 St.
Tom's, 418 McRae St.
Crosby's , Dial 9246
Greyhound, Dial 2-1342
TAILORS
New Progressive, 525 Red Cross St.

OHIO
AKRON
HOTELS
Green Turtle, Federal & Howard
Garden City, Howard & Furnace
Matthews, 77 N. Howard St.
TOURIST HOMES
R. Wilson, 370 Robert St.
BARBER SHOPS
Goodwill's, 422 Robert St.
Matthew's, 77 N. Howard St.
Allen's, 43 N. Howard St.
TAVERNS
Garden City, 124 N. Howard St.
SERVICE STATIONS
Dunagan, 834 Rhoades Ave.
ALLIANCE
TOURIST HOMES
Mrs. W. Jackson, 774 N. Webb Ave.
CADIZ
TOURIST HOMES
Mrs. James Pettress, RFD 2
CANTON
HOTELS
Phillis Wheatly Asso., 612 Market Ave. So.
DRUG STORES
Southside, 503 Cherry Ave., S. E.

CINCINNATI

HOTELS
Y.W.C.A., 702 W. 8th St.
Manse, 1004 Chapel St.

TOURIST HOMES
O. Steele, 3065 Kerper St.
Ethel Buckner, 505 W. 8th St.

RESTAURANTS
Miniature Grill, 1132 Chapel St.
Mom's, 6th & John Sts.
Perkins, 430 W. 5th St.
Loc-Fre, 1634 Freeman St.
Williams, 1053 Freeman St.
Hide Away, 524 W. 5th St.
Hill's, 645 Richmond St.
Naomi's, 667 Linn St.
Harry Bruce, 404 W. 5th St.
Helen Johnson, 622 Mound St.
Ida Miller, 611 W. 6th St.
Felix Savage, George & John St.
Wm. Taylor's, 400 W. Court St.

CHINESE RESTAURANTS
Tim Pang, 514 W. 6th St.

BEAUTY PARLORS
Neighborhood, 927 Linn St.
Efficiency, 878 Beecher St.
Mill's, 2639 Park Ave.
E. N. Anderson, 1533 Blair Ave.
E. Anderson, 701 Cutter St.
Carrie Brown, 749 W. Court St.
Breck's, 1569½ Central Ave.
Margaret Brown, 924 Linn St.
Cleaver Mae's, 1018 John St.
Rosebud, 713 W. Court St.
Ludie's, 444 Chestnut St.
Pattie Lounds, 927 Linn St.
Mrs. Mahan, 551 W. Liberty St.
Margaret Peak, 2614 Park Ave.
Callie P. Smith, 709 Mound St.
Martha Williams, 506 W. 5th St.
B. Wilkins, 639 Richmond St.

BARBER SHOPS
5th Ave., 528 W. 5th Ave.
Clifford Brown, 1213 Linn St.
R. E. Crump, 500 W. 6th St.
George Cannon, 434 W. 5th St.
C. Lewis Handy, 810 John St.
Rev. Wm. Halbert, 703 Kenyon Ave.
Charles Humphrey, 528 W. 5th St.
Flowers Slaughter, 435 W. 5th St.

TAVERNS
Travelers Inn, 1115 Hopkins St.
Log Cabin, 608 John St.
Kitty Kat, 417 W. 5th St.
Barr & Linn, 760 Barr St.
Shuffle Inn, 638 Baymiller St.
Wright's, 776 W. 5th St.
Ben, 723 W. 5th St.
Silver Fleet, 810 W. 8th St.
Felder's, 810 W. 8th St.
Hotel, 542 W. 7th St.

DRUG STORES
Sky Pharmacy, 5th & John Sts.
Hoard's, 937 Central Ave.

Fallon's, 6th & Mound Sts.
West End, 709 W. Court St.
Mangrum, Chapel & Park Ave.
Dr. Russel, 612 W. 9th St.

NIGHT CLUBS
Cotton Club, 6th & Mound St.
Downbeat, Beecher & Gilbert Sts.

ROAD HOUSES
Shuffle Inn, 7th & Carr Sts.

TAILORS
De Luxe, 1217 Linn St.
Charles Bell, 603 W. 6th St.
Walthal, 732 W. 5th St.

SERVICE STATIONS
S. & W., 9th & Mound Sts.
Coursey, 2985 Gilbert Ave.
9th St., 9th & Mound St.

TAXI CABS
Calvin, 9th & Mound Sts.

CLEVELAND

HOTELS

Ward's Apartment Hotel
4113 Cedar Ave.
Ward, 4113 Cedar Ave.
Phyllis Wheatly, 4300 Cedar Ave.
Carnegie, 6803 Carnegie Ave.
Geraldine, 2212 E. 40th St.
Y.M.C.A., E. 76th & Cedar
Majestic, 2291 E. 55th St.

TOURIST HOMES
Mrs. Fannie Gilmer, 10519 Kimberley Ave.
Mrs. Edith Wilkins, 2121 E. 46th

RESTAURANTS
Williams, Central & E. 49th St.
Cassie's, 2284 E. 55th St.
Manhattan, 9903 Cedar Ave.
State, 7817 Cedar

BEAUTY PARLORS
Alberta's, 8203 Cedar Ave.
Wilkin's, 12813 Kinsman Rd.

BARBER SHOPS
Bryant's, 9805 Cedar Ave.
Driskill, 1243 E. 105th St.

TAVERNS
Brown Derby, 40th & Woodland Ave
Cedar Gardens, 9706 Cedar Ave.
Cafe Society, 966 E. 105th St.
Gold Bar, 105th St. & Massic Ave.

NIGHT CLUBS
Douglas, 7917 Cedar Ave.

BEAUTY CULTURE SCHOOLS
Wilkins, 2112 E. 46th St.

SERVICE STATIONS
Kyer's, Cedar & 79th St.
Amoco, 1416 E. 105th St.

DRUG STORES
Benjamin's, E. 55th St. & Central

TAILORS
Grant's, 9502 Cedar Ave.

COLUMBUS
HOTELS

HOTEL ST. CLAIR
Service and Comfort Is Our Motto
Completely Air Conditioned
Dining Room Service - Elevator, Valet
Laundry - Telegraph
A. J. McKibbon, *Manager*
338-46 ST. CLAIR AVE.
Tel.: Fairfax 1181-2-3

___

Hotel St. Clair
338 St. Clair Ave.
Phone: Fairfax 1181-82-83
Ford, 179 N. 6th St.
Lexington, 180 Lexington Ave.
Macon Hotel, 366 N. 20th St.
Charlton, 439 Hamilton Ave.
Hawkins, 65 N. Monroe Ave.
Litchferd, N. 4th St.
Newford, 452½ E. Long St.
Deshler-Wallick, Board & High Sts.
Fort Hayes, 31 W. Spring St.
Garden Manor, 91 Miami Ave.
Neil House, 415 High St.
St. Clair, 338 St. Clair Ave.
TOURIST HOMES
Hawkins, 70 N. Monroe Ave.
Cooper, 259 N. 17th St.
RESTAURANTS
Cottage Restaurant & Sandwich
Shop, 540 N. 20th St.
B. & B., 318 Barthman Ave.
Southern Tea Room, 618 Long St.
Bruce Latham, 317 Hosacks St.
Belmont, 689 E. Long St.
Turner's, 452½ E. Long
Edward's, 318 Barthman Ave.
Atcheson, 1288 Atcheson St.
Duck Inn, 382 E. 5th St.
Bessie's, 423 W. Goodale St.
TAVERNS
Mickey's, 425 Goodale St.
Lincoln, 389 W. Goodale St.
Royal, 752 E. Long St.
Paradise, 878 Mt. Vernon Ave.
Duck Inn, 382 E. 5th Ave.
Novelty, 741 E. Long St.
Poinciana, 758 E. Long St.
Village, 1219 Mt. Vernon Ave.
NIGHT CLUBS
Club Rogue, 772½ E. Long St.
Belmont, 659 Long St.
Skurdy's, 1074 Mt. Vernon Ave.
Club 169, Cleveland Ave.
Club Regal, 772 E. Long St.
Yatch, Cor. 20th & Mt. Vernon
McCown's, St. Clair & Mt. Vernon
BEAUTY PARLORS
Evelyn's, 947 Mt. Vernon Ave.
Long's, Charlie Mae's, 925 Mt.
Vernon Ave.

Helena's, 336 Carsons Ave.
Vi's, 281 N. 18th St.
The Ave. Beauty Shop, 881 Mt.
Vernon
Shingle House, 1409 Granville St.
Our Beauty Shop, 1163 Atcheson
The Classics, 925 Mt. Vernon Ave.
Justa Mere Beauty Shop, 345 N.
20th.
Ola's, 434 N. Monroe Ave.
Elaum's, 172 Lexington Ave.
Mond's Classic, 920 E. Long St.
BARBER SHOPS
Sugg & Bennie, 621 Long St.
Whaley's, 614 E. Long St.
Pierce's, 483 E. Long St.
GARAGES
Smith's, 492 Charles St.
AUTOMOTIVE
Brooks, 466 S. Washington St.
SERVICE STATIONS
King's, E. Long & Monroe
Peyton Sohio's, E. Long & Monroe
Brook's, 466 S. Washington Ave.

DAYTON
HOTELS
Y.M.C.A., 907 W. 5th St.
TOURIST HOMES
B. Lawrence, 206 Norwood St.
RESTAURANTS
TAVERNS
Palmer House, 1107 Germantown
SERVICE STATIONS
Poorer's, Shio, 1200 W. 5th St.

LIMA
TOURIST HOMES
Sol Downton, 1124 W. Spring St.
Edward Holt, 406 E. High St.
Mrs. A. Turner, 1215 W. Spring St.
George Cook, 230 S. Union St.
BEAUTY PARLORS
Nancy's, 1431 Norval Ave.

LORAIN
TOURIST HOMES
Mrs. Alex Cooley, 114 W. 26th St.
Mrs. W. H. Redmond, 201 E. 22nd
Worthington, 209 W. 16th St.
Porter Wood, 1759 Broadway
H. P. Jackson, 2383 Apple Ave.
INNS
Wood's Social Inn
Beer, Wine, Food & Liquor
1759 Broadway

MANSFIELD
HOTELS
Lincoln, 757 N. Bowman St.
DRUG STORES
Mayer, 243 N. Main St.

MARIETTA
TOURIST HOMES
Mrs. E. Jackson, 213 Church St.

56

MIDDLETOWN
RESTAURANTS
TAILORS
Tramell, 1308 Garfield

OBERLIN
HOTELS
Oberlin Inn, College & Main

SANDUSKY
HOTELS
Hunter, 407 W. Market St.
BARBER SHOPS
Peoples, 218 W. Water St.

SPRINGFIELD
HOTELS
Posey, 269 S. Fountain Ave.
Y.M.C.A., Center St.
Y.W.C.A., Clarke St.
TOURIST HOMES
Mrs. M. E. Wilborn, 220 Fair St.
RESTAURANTS
Posey, 211 S. Fountain Ave.
BEAUTY PARLORS
Powder Puff, 638 S. Wittenberg Ave.
BARBER SHOPS
Griffith & Martin, 127 S. Center St.
Harris, 39 W. Clark St.
TAVERNS
Posey's, 211 S. Fountain Ave.
NIGHT CLUBS
K. P. Imp. Club, S. Yellow Spring
SERVICE STATIONS
Underwood, 1303 S. Yellow Spring
GARAGES
Green's, 1371 W. Pleasant St.
Ben's, 935 Sherman Ave.

TOLEDO
HOTELS
Pleasant, 15 N. Erie Ave.
TOURIST HOMES
Cook's Tourist Home
1736-38 Washington St.
G. Davis, 532 Woodland Ave.
Mrs. J. Jennings, 729 Indiana Ave.
J. F. Watson, 399 Pinewood Ave.
P. Johnson, 1102 Collingwood Blvd.
Cook's, 1736 Washington St.

COOK'S TOURIST HOME
"Toledo's Finest"
Fans, Radios, Air Conditioners in Most Rooms
1736-38 WASHINGTON ST.
Tel.: Emerson 1640

BARBER SHOPS
Chiles, Indiana & Collingwood
TAVERNS
Indiana, 529 Indiana Ave.
Midway, 764 Tecumsik St.
SERVICE STATIONS
Darling's, 835 Pinewood Ave.
Hobb's, 714 Palmwood

YOUNGSTOWN
HOTELS
Hotel Allison
212 North West Ave.
Y.M.C.A., 362 W. Federal St.
Rideuot, 383 Lincoln Ave.
McDonald, 442 E. Federal
Royal Palms, 625 Hemrod
Gold Inn, 851 W. Federal
Mohoning, 3411 Nelson Ave.
TOURIST HOMES
Belmont, 327 Belmont Ave.
RESTAURANTS
"Y," 962 Federal St.
Central, 137 S. Center
Bagnet, 316 Covington
BARBER SHOPS
Harris, 701 W. Rayen Ave.
BEAUTY PARLORS
Renee's, 321 E. Federal St.
Francine, 427 W. Chicago Ave.
TAVERNS
Sponteno, 377 E. Federal
State, 130 E. Broadman
TAILORS
H. V. Walker, 371 E. Federal
GARAGES
Underwood, 543 5th Ave.
NIGHT CLUBS
40 Club, 399 E. Federal St.
40 Club, 369 E. Federal
West Side Social, 552 W. Federal
A. A. Social, 703 W. Rayen Ave.

ZANESVILLE
HOTELS
Park, 1561 W. Main St.
RESTAURANTS
Little Harlem, Lee St.
TOURIST HOMES
L. E. Costom, 1545 N. Main St.
BARBER SHOPS
Nap Love, Second St.

OKLAHOMA
BOLEY
HOTELS
Berry's, South Main St.

CHICKASHA
TOURIST HOMES
Boyd's, 1022 Shepard St.

ENID
TOURIST HOMES
Mrs. Eliza Baty, 520 E. State St.
Mrs. Johnson, 217 E. Market St.
Edward's, 223 E. Park St.

GUTHRIE
TOURIST HOMES
James, 1002 E. Springer Ave.
Mrs. M. A. Smith, 317 E. Second St.

57

MUSKOGEE

HOTELS
People's, 316 N. 2nd St.
Elliots, 111½ So. 2nd St.
RESTAURANTS
People's, 316 N. 2nd St.
BARBER SHOPS
Central, 228 N. Second St.
Robbins, 114 Court St.
BEAUTY PARLORS
Lenora's, 228 N. 2nd St.
SERVICE STATIONS
Smith's, 228 N. 2nd St.
AUTOMOTIVE
Smith Tire Co., 2nd & Denison Sts.
GARAGES
Middleton's, 420 N. 2nd St.
Nelson's, 940 S. 20th St.
London's, 209 Denison
TAILORS
Williams, 321 N. 2nd St.
Ezell's, 208 S. 2nd St.

OKLAHOMA CITY

HOTELS
4th St. Branch Y.M.C.A.
614 N.E. 4th St.
Y.M.C.A., 614 N. E. 4th St.
Canton, 200 N. E. 2nd St.
Little Page, 219 N. Central
Littlepage Hotel
219 N. Central St.
Phone: Regent 9-8779
Hall, 205½ N. Central
TOURIST HOMES
Scrugg's, 420 N. Laird St.
Cortland Rms., 629 N. E. 4th St.
Tucker's, 315½ N. E. 2nd St.
Mrs. Lessie Bennett, 500 N. E. 4th
RESTAURANTS
Eastside Food Shop, 904 N. E. 2nd
BEAUTY PARLORS
W. B. Ellis, 505 N. E. 5th St.
Lyons, 316 North Central
BARBER SHOPS
Golden Oak, 300 Block N. E. 2nd
Clover Leaf, 300 Block N. E. 2nd
SERVICE STATIONS
Richardson's, 400 N. E. 2nd St.
Mathues, 1023 N. E. 4th St.
DRUG STORES
Randolph, 331 N. E. 2nd St.

OKMULGEE

RESTAURANTS
Simmons, 407 E. 5th St.
TAXI CABS
H. & H., 421 E. 5th St.

SHAWNEE

HOTELS
Olison, 501 S. Bell St.
Slugg's, 410 So. Bell St.
TOURIST HOMES
M. Gross, 602 S. Bell St.

TULSA

HOTELS
Avalon, 2411 Apache St.
Y.W.C.A., 1120 East Pine
Lafayette, 604 E. Archer St.
McHunt, 1121 N. Greenwood Ave.
Small, 615 E. Archer
Del Rio, 607½ N. Greenwood
Miller, 124 N. Hartford St.
TOURIST HOMES
W. H. Smith, 124½ N. Greenwood
C. U. Netherland, 542 N. Elgin St.
RESTAURANTS
Chicken Shack, 316 N. Elgin
Art's Chili Parlor, 110 N. Greenwood
The Upstairs Dining Rm. 119½ N. Greenwood
BEAUTY PARLORS
Eula's, 205 N. Greenwood
BARBER SHOPS
Swindall's, 203 N. Greenwood
TAILORS
Lawson, 1120 Greenwood Ave.
Carver's, 125 N. Greenwood Ave.
SERVICE STATIONS
Mince, 2nd & Elgin Sts.
DRUGS
Mebarry Drugs, 101 Greenwood St.

OREGON

PORTLAND

HOTELS
Medley, 2272 N. Interstate Ave.
Y.W.C.A., N. E. Williams Ave. & Till.
RESTAURANTS
Barno's, 84 N. E. Broadway
BEAUTY PARLORS
Bakers, 6525 N. E. Grand Ave.
Redmond, 2862 S. E. Ankeny
Mott Sisters, 2107 Vancouver Ave.
BARBER SHOPS
Holliday's, 511 N. W. 6th Ave.
NIGHT CLUBS
Oregon Fat., 1412 N. Wms.
ROAD HOUSES
Spicers, 1734 N. William Ave.
TAXI CABS
Broadway DeLuxe Cab, Br. 1-2-3-4

PENNSYLVANIA

ALLENTOWN

RESTAURANTS
Southern, 372 Union St.

ALTOONA

TOURIST HOMES
C. Bell, 1420 Wash. Ave.
Mrs. E. Jackson, 2138 18th St.
Mrs. H. Shorter, 2620 8th St.

BEDFORD SPRINGS
HOTELS
Harris Hotel, Penn. & West Sts.

CHAMBERSBURG
TOURIST HOME
Pinn's, 68 W. Liberty St.

COATESVILLE
HOTELS
Subway

CHESTER
HOTELS
Harlem, 1909 W. 3rd St.
Moonglow, 225 Market St.
BEAUTY PARLORS
Rosella, 413 Concord Ave.
Alex. Davis, 123 Reaney St.
BARBER SHOPS
Bouldin, 1710 W. 3rd St.
TAVERNS
Wright's, 3rd St. & Central Ave.

CRESCO
TOURIST HOMES
Mrs. Daniel L. Taylor

DARBY
TAVERNS
Golden Star, 10th & Forrester

ERIE
HOTELS
Pope, 1318 French St.

GETTYSBURG
TOURIST HOMES

GERMANTOWN
HOTELS
Y.M.C.A., 132 W. Rittenhouse
TAVERNS
Terrace Grill, 75 E. Sharpnack St.

HARRISBURG
HOTELS
Jackson, 1004 N. 6th St.
Jack's, 1208 N. 6th St.
TOURIST HOMES
Mrs. W. D. Jones, 1531 No. 6th St.
Mrs. H. Carter, 606 Foster St.
BARBER SHOPS
Jack's, 1002 N. 6th St.

LANCASTER
BEAUTY PARLORS
E. Clark, 505 S. Duke St.
J. Carter, 143 S. Duke St.
A. L. Polite, 540 North St.

NEW CASTLE
HOTELS
Y.W.C.A., 140 Elm St.

OIL CITY
TOURIST HOMES
Mrs. Jackson, 258 Bissel Ave.

PHILADELPHIA
HOTELS
Southwest Y.W.C.A., Res.
756 S. 16th St.

Paradise, 1527 Fitzwater St.
Bellevue-Stratford, Broad & Walnut
Benjamin Franklin, 9th & Chestnut Sts.
Essex House, 13th & Fillbert Sts.
Chesterfield, Broad & Oxford Sts.
Baltimore, 1438 Lombard St.
Attucks, 801 S. 15th St.
Elizabeth, 756 S. 15th St.
Woodson, 1414 Lombard
The Grand, 420 So. 15th St.
Douglas, Broad & Lombard Sts.
Elrae, 805 N. 13th St.
LaSalle, 2026 Ridge Ave.
New Roadside, 514 S. 15th St.
Paradise, 1527 Fitzwater St.
Y.M.C.A., 1724 Christian St.
Y.W.C.A., 1605 Catherine St.
Y.W.C.A., 6128 Germantown Ave.
Horseshoe, 12th & Lombard
New Phain, 2059 Fitzwater
La Reve, Cor. 9th & Columbia Ave.
Ridge, 1610 Ridge Ave.
Pitts, 1301 Poplar St.
Carlyle, 1425 W. Poplar St.
Doris, 2219 N. 13th St.
RESTAURANTS
Marion's, 20th & Bainbridge Sts.
Trott Inn, 5030 Haverford Ave.
Mattie's, 4225 Pennsgrove St.
Ruth's, 1848 N. 17th St.
BEAUTY PARLORS
A. Henson, 1318 Fairmont Ave.
LaSalle, 2036 Ridge St.
Lady Ross, 718 S. 15th St.
Rose's, 16th & South St.
F. Franklin, 2115 W. York St.
Motom's, 816 So. 15th St.
Redmond's, 4823 Fairmont Ave.
A. B. Tooks, 1702 Diamond St.
SCHOOL OF BEAUTY CULTURE
Carter's School, 1811 W. Columbia
BARBER SHOPS
S. Jones, 1423 Ridge Ave.
TAVERNS
Irene's, 2345 London Ave.
Trott Inn, 5030 Haverford Ave.
Wander Inn, 18th & Federal St.
Butler's Tavern, 17th & Carpenter
Campbell's, 18th & South St.
Loyal, 16th & South Sts.
Irene's, 2329 Ridge Ave.
Lyons, 12th & South St.
Blue Moon, 1702 Federal St.
Butler's, 2666 Ridge Ave.
Cotton Grove, 1329 South St.
Wayside Inn, 13th & Oxford St.
Preston's, 4043 Market St.
Casbah, 39th & Fairmont St.
Last Word, Haverford & 51st St.
Cathrine's, 1350 South St.
Postal Card, 1504 South St.
Emerson's, 15th & Bainbridge St.
Brass Rail, 2302 W. Columbia Ave.
Club 421, 5601 Wyalusing Ave.

NIGHT CLUBS
Cotton Club, 2106 Ridge Ave.
Cafe Society, 1306 W. Columbia Ave.
Paradise, Ridge & Jefferson
Progressive, 1415 S. 20th St.
Cotton Bowl, Master St. & 13th St.

GARAGES
Bond Motor Service, 6726 N. 8th St.
Booker Bros., 1245 So. 21st St.

SERVICE STATIONS
Witcher, 1856 No. Judson St.

DRUG STORES
Bound's, 59th & Race St.

PITTSBURGH

HOTELS
Flamingo, 2407 Wylie Ave.
Ave., 1538 Wylie Ave.
Bailey's, 1533 Center Ave.
Colonial, Wylie & Fulton Sts.
Palace, 1545 Wylie Ave.
Ellis, 5 Reed St.

TOURIST HOMES
Agnes Taylor, 2612 Center St.
Birdie's Guest House, 1522 Center Ave.
B. Williams, 1537 Howard St.
Mrs. Williams, 5518 Claybourne St.

RESTAURANTS
Dearling's, 492 Culver St.
Vee's Dining Room, 2403 Centre Ave.

READING

TOURIST HOMES
C. Dawson, 441 Buttonwood St.

SCRANTON

TOURIST HOMES
Mrs. Elvira R. King,
1312 Linden St.
Mrs. J. Taylor, 1415 Penn. Ave.

SELLERSVILLE

TOURIST HOMES
Mrs. Dorothy Scholls, Forest Rd.

SHARON HILL

TAVERNS
Dixie Cafe, Hook Rd., Howard St.

WASHINGTON

TOURIST HOMES
Richardson, 140 E. Chestnut St.

RESTAURANTS
W. Allen, N. Lincoln St.
M. Thomas, N. Lincoln St.

BARBER SHOPS
Yancey's, E. Spruce St.

NIGHT CLUBS
Thomas Grill, N. Lincoln St.

WAYNE

NIGHT CLUBS
Plantation, Gulf Rd. & Henry Ave.

WESTCHESTER
Magnolia, 300 E. Miner St.

WILLIAMSPORT

TOURIST HOMES
Mrs. Edward Randall, 719 Matle St.

WILKES BARRE

HOTELS
Shaw, 15 So. State St.

YORK

TOURIST HOMES
Mrs. I. Grayson, 32 W. Princess St

RHODE ISLAND
NEWPORT

TOURIST HOMES
Ma Gruber, 82 William St.
Mrs. F. Jackson, 28 Hall Ave.
Mrs. L. Jackson, 35 Bath Rd.

PROVIDENCE

HOTELS
Biltmore

TOURIST HOMES
Hines, 462 North Main St.
Retlaw House, 24 Camp St.

TAVERNS
Dixieland, 1049 Westminster St

BEAUTY PARLORS
B. Boyd's, 43 Camp St.
Geraldine's, 205 Thurbus Ave.

SOUTH CAROLINA
ANDERSON

RESTAURANTS
Ess-Tee, 112 E. Church St.

TOURIST HOMES
Mrs. Sallie Galloway, 420 Butler St.

AIKEN

TOURIST HOMES
C. F. Holland, 1118 Richland Ave.

ATLANTIC BEACH

HOTELS
Theretha

BEAUFORD

SERVICE STATIONS
Peoples, D. Brofn, Prop.

CHARLESTON

TOURIST HOMES
Mrs. Gladsen, 15 Nassau St.
Mrs. Mayes, 82½ Spring St.

CHERAW

TOURIST HOMES
Mrs. M. B. Robinson, 211 Church
Mrs. Maggie Green, Church St.
Liveoak, 328 2nd St.

RESTAURANTS
College Inn,
324 2nd St.
Gate Grill, 2nd St.
Watson, 2nd St.

TAVERNS
College Inn, 2nd St.

ROAD HOUSES
Hill Top, Society Hill Rd.
BARBER SHOPS
Imperial, 276 2nd St.
BEAUTY PARLORS
Bell's, Huger St.
SERVICE STATIONS
Motor Inn, 2nd St.

COLA

BEAUTY PARLORS
Workman's, 1825 Taylor St.

COLUMBIA

HOTELS
Y.W.C.A., 1429 Park St.
Nylon, 918 Senate St.
TOURIST HOMES
Mrs. Irene B. Evans, 1106 Pine St.
College Inn, 1609 Harden St.
Mrs. S. H. Smith, 929 Pine St.
Mrs. H. Cornwell, 1713 Wayne
Mrs. W. D. Chappelle, 1301 Pine St.
Beachum, 2212 Gervais St.
Mrs. J. F. Wakefield 816 Oak St.
RESTAURANTS
Green Leaf, 1117 Wash. St.
Savoy, Old Winnsboro St.
Cozy Inn, 1509 Harden St.
Mom's, 1005 Washington St.
Brown's, 1014 Lady St.
Blue Palace, 1001 Washington St.
Waverly, 2515 Gervais St.
BEAUTY PARLORS
Amy's, 1125½ Washington St.
Obbie's, 119½ Washington St.
BARBER SHOPS
Holman's, 2138 Gervais St.
BEAUTY SCHOOLS
Poro, 2481 Millwood Ave.
Madare Bradley, 2228 Hampton St.
TAVERNS
Moon Glow, 1005 Washington St.
SERVICE STATIONS
A. W. Simkins, 1331 Park St.
Caldwell's, Oak & Taylor Sts.
Waverly, 2202 Taylor St.
Leevy's, 1831 Taylor St.
DRUG STORES
Count's, 1105 Washington St.
TAXI CABS
Blue Ribbon, 1024 Washington St.

CROSS HILL

RESTAURANTS
Willie Miller

FLORENCE

TOURIST HOMES

You're Always Welcome at

EBONY GUEST HOUSE

FLORENCE'S FAMOUS GUEST
HOUSE
Your Home—Away from Home
712 NO. WILSON ST.
Florence, S. C.

Richmond, 108 S. Griffin St.
John McDonald, 501 So. Irby St.
Mrs. B. Wright, 1004 E. Cheeve St.
RESTAURANTS
Ace's Grill, 114 E. Cheeve St.
Wright's, 110 S. Griffin St.

GEORGETOWN

TOURIST HOMES
Mrs. R. Anderson, 424 Broad
Mrs. D. Atkinson, 811 Duke
Jas. Becote, 118 Orange
T. W. Brown, Merriman & Emanuel
Mrs. A. A. Smith, 317 Emanuel

GREENVILLE

TOURIST HOMES
Dr. Gibbs, 914 Anderson Rd.
Miss M. J. Grimes, 210 Mean St.
Mrs. W. H. Smith, 212 John St.
RESTAURANTS
Fowlers, 16 Spring St.
BEAUTY PARLORS
Broadway, 11 Spring St.
BARBER SHOPS
Broadway, 8 Spring St.
GARAGES
Whittenburg, 600 Anderson St.
PHARMACY
Gibbs, 101 E. Broad St.

MULLINS

TOURIST HOMES
E. Calhoun's, 535 N. Smith St.
BARBER SHOPS
Noham Ham, Front St.
NIGHT CLUBS
Calhoun Nite Club, 535 Smith St.
ROAD HOUSES
Kate Odom, 76 H'way
SERVICE STATIONS
Ed. Owins', Front St.

ORANGEBURG

DRUG STORES
Danzier, 121 W. Russell St.

SPARTANBURG

TOURIST HOMES
Mrs. O. Jones, 255 N. Dean St.
Mrs. L. Johnson, 307 N. Dean
RESTAURANTS
Mrs. M. Davis, S. Wofford
BEAUTY PARLORS
Clowney's, 445 S. Liberty St.
BARBER SHOPS
R. Browning, 122 Short Wofford
TAVERNS
Victory, Union Highway
SERVICE STATIONS
Collins, 398 S. Liberty St.
South Side, S. Liberty St.
TAXI CABS
Collin's, 389 S. Liberty St.

ROCK HILL
BEAUTY SCHOOLS
Jefferson's, 168 W. Black St.
SUMTER
TOURIST HOMES
Edmonia Shaw, 206 Manning Ave.
Mrs. Julia E. Byrd, 504 N. Main
C. H. Bracey, 210 W. Oakland
Johnnie Williams, Hi'way 15A
TAVERNS
Steve Bradford, N. Main St.
SERVICE STATIONS
Esso Gas Station
Mutual, 208 Bartlee St.
DRUG STORES
People, 5 W. Liberty St.
WALTERBORO
TOURIST HOMES
Mrs. Rebecca Maree, 14 Savage St.
RESTAURANTS
Keynote, Gruber St.

SOUTH DAKOTA
ABERDEEN
HOTELS
Alonzo Ward, S. Main St.
RESTAURANTS
Virginia, 303 S. Main St .
BEAUTY PARLORS
Marland, 321 S. Main St.
BARBER SHOPS
Olson, 103½ S. Main St.
SERVICE STATIONS
Swanson, H'way 12 & Main Sts.
GARAGES
Spaulding, S. Lincoln St.
Wallace, S. Lincoln St.
SIOUX FALLS
TOURIST HOMES
Mrs. J. Moxley, 915 N. Main
Chamber of Commerce, 131 S.
Phillips Ave.

TENNESSEE
BRISTOL
TOURIST HOMES
Mrs. M. C. Brown, 225 McDowell
Mrs. A. D. Henderson, 301
McDowell St.
TAVERNS
The Morocco, 800 Spencer St.
CHATTANOOGA
HOTELS
Y.M.C.A., 793 E. 9th St.
Dallas, 230½ E. 9th St.
Lincoln, 1101 Carter St.
Martin, 204 E. 9th St.
Peoples, 1104 Carter St.
Dallas, 230½ E. 9th St.
Harris, 110½ Carter St.

TOURIST HOMES
Mrs. Etta Brown, 1129 E. 8th St.
Mrs. J. Baker, 843 E. 8th St.
Y.W.C.A., 839 E. 8th St.
J. Carter, 1022 E. 8th St.
RESTAURANTS
Thomas Chicken Shack, 235 E.
9th St.
La Grand, 205 E. 9th St.
Manhattan, 324 E. 9th St.
Brown Derby, 331 E. 9th St.
TAVERNS
Gamble's, 108 W. Main St.
Brown Derby, 331 E. 9th St.
Dandy's, 1101 W. 12th St.
Mrs. Annie Ruth Conley, 205 E.
9th St.
LIQUOR STORES
Pat's, 727 James Blgd.
Walter Johnson, 213 E. 8th St.
Cap's, 422 E. 9th St.
Watt's, 320 E. 9th St.
DRUG STORES
Rowland's, 326 E. 9th St.
Moore & King, 836 Market St.
GARAGES
Volunteer, E. 9th St. & Lindsay
TAXI CABS
Simms, 915 University Ave.
CLARKSVILLE
TOURIST HOMES
Mrs. H. Northington, 717 Main St.
Mrs. Kate Stewart, 500 Poston St.
RESTAURANTS
Foston's Grill,
853 College St.
Foston's, 853 College St.
BEAUTY PARLORS
Johnson's, 10th St.
KNOXVILLE
Y.W.C.A., 329 Temperance St.
Hartford, 219 ... Vine St.
TOURIST HOMES
Rollins, 302 E. Vine St.
Anderson's, 501 E. Church St.
RESTAURANTS

LEXINGTON

TOURIST HOMES
C. Timberlake, Holly St.

MEMPHIS

HOTELS
Marguette Hotel, 500 Linden St.
Travelers, 347 Vance
Mitchells, 160 Hernando St.
Larraine, Mulberry At Huling
Eosary, 181 Beale Ave.
TOURIST HOMES
Mrs. E. M. Wright, 896 Polk Ave.
RESTAURANTS
Scott's, 368 Vance Ave.
Davidson's, 345 S. 4th St.
Bessie's, 238 Vance Ave.
NIGHT CLUBS
Tony's Place, 1404 Lyceum Rd.
BEAUTY SCHOOLS
Burchitta, 201 Hernando St.
Superior, 1550 Florida Ave.
Johnson, 316 S. 4th St.
DRUG STORES
So. Memphis, 907 Florida Ave.
Pantaza, Main & Beale

MURFREESBORO

TOURIST HOMES
Mrs. M. E. Howland, 439 E. State

NASHVILLE

HOTELS
Y.M.C.A., 4th & Charlotte Aves.
Grace, 1122 Cedar St.
Carver Courts, White's, Creek Pike
Y.W.C.A., 436 5th Ave. N.
Brown's, 1610 Jefferson St., North
Bryant House, 500 8th Ave. So.
BEAUTY PARLORS
Queen of Sheba, 1503 15th Ave., N.
Myrtles, 2423 Eden St.
BEAUTY SCHOOLS
Bowman's, 409 4th Ave., N.
RESTAURANTS
Martha's, 309 Cedar St.
Peacock Inn, Jefferson & 18th Ave.
BARBER SHOPS
'Y', 34 4th Ave. N.

TEXAS

ABILENE

TAVERNS
Hammond Cafe, 620 Plum St.

AMARILLO

HOTELS
Watley, 112 Van Buren St.
Tennessee, 206 Van Buren St.
RESTAURANTS
Tom's Place, 322 W. Third St.
New Harlem, 114 Harrison St.
BARBER SHOPS
Foster's, 204 Harrison St.

BEAUTY PARLORS
Unique, 312 W. Third St.
ROAD HOUSES
Working Man's Club, 202 Harrison
TAVERNS
Carter Bros., 323 W. Third St.
TAILORS
Mitchell's, 314 W. Second St.
RECREATION CLUBS
Blue Moon, 107 Harrison St.
Watley, 202 Harrison St.
DRUG STORES
G. & M. 204A Harrison St.
Knighton, 422 W. Third St.
Corner, 118 Harrison St.

ATLANTA

TOURIST HOMES
Mrs. Lizzie Simon, 308 N. Howe St.

AUSTIN

TOURIST HOMES
Mrs. J. W. Frazier, 810 E. 13th St.
Mrs. J. W. Duncan, 1214 E. 7th St.
Mrs. W. M. Tears, 1203 E. 12th St.
Porter's, 1315 E. 12th St.

BEAUMONT

HOTELS
Whitney, 2997 Pine St.
Hotel Theresa, 875 Neches St.
TOURIST HOMES
Mrs. Pearl Freeman, 730 Forsythe
Mrs. B. Rivers, 730 Forsythe St.
RESTAURANTS
Long Bar-B-Q, 539 Forsythe St.

CORPUS CHRISTIE

TOURIST HOMES
Horace Crecy's, 1710 Lexington Ave.
RESTAURANTS
Avalon, 1510 Ramirez
Skylark, 1216 N. Staples
Blue Willow, 806 Winnebago
Square Deal, 810 Winnebago
Royal, 1222 N. Staples St.
Fortuna, 1307 N. Staples St.
BEAUTY PARLORS
Mitchell's, 1519 Ramirez St.
Bessie's, 1526½ Sam Rankin
BARBER SHOPS
Steen's, 1303 N. Alameda St.
NIGHT CLUBS
Alabam, 1503 Ramirez
Elite, 1216 N. Staples St.
LIQUOR STORES
Savoy, 1220 N. Staples St.
GARAGES
Crecy's, 1502 Ramirez

CORSICANA

TOURIST HOMES
Mrs. R. Lee, 712 E. 4th St.
BARBER SHOPS
Mrs. Dellum, 117 E. 5th Ave.

DALLAS

HOTELS
Howard Hotel
3118 San Jacinto St.
Phone: Ta 5970
Lewis, 302½ N. Central St.
Powell, 3115 State St.
Y.M.C.A., 2700 Flora St.
Y.W.C.A., 3525 State St.
Hall's, 1825½ Hall St.
RESTAURANTS
Shalimar Grill,
2219 Hall St.
Beaumont Barbeque, 1815 N. Field
Davis, 6806 Lemmon Ave.
Palm Cafe, 2213 Hall St.
BEAUTY PARLORS
S. Brown's, 1721 Hall St.
BARBER SHOPS
Washington's, 3203 Thomas Ave.
DRUG STORES
Smith's, 2221 Hall St.

EL PASO

HOTELS
Phillips Manor, 218 So. Mesa
Murray Theater, 218 S. Mesa Ave.
Daniel Hotel, 413 S. Oregon St.
TOURIST HOMES
A. Winston, 3205 Almeda St.
Mrs. S. W. Stull, 511 Tornillo
C. Williams, 1507 Wyoming St.
E. Phillips, 704 S. St. Vrain St.
DRUG STORES
Donnel, 3201 Nanzana St.

FORT WORTH

HOTELS
Del Ray, 901 Jones St.
Jim, 413-15 E. Fifth St.
TOURIST HOMES
Evan's, 1213 E. Terrell St.
RESTAURANTS
Y.M.C.A., 1604 Jones St.
Green Leaf, 315 E. 9th St.
BEAUTY PARLORS
Dickerson's, 1015 E. Rosedale
SERVICE STATIONS
South Side, 1151 New York St.

GALVESTON

HOTELS
Oleander, 421½ 25th St.
Gus Allen, 2710 Ave. F.
TOURIST HOMES
Mrs. J. Pope, 2824 Ave. M.
TAVERNS
Gulf View, 28th & Blvd. Houston
NIGHT CLUBS
Manhattan, 2802 Ave. R½
BARBER SHOPS
Imperial, 1814-O½
GARAGES
Sunset, 3928 Ave. H.

HENDERSON

RESTAURANTS
Chat & Chew, 615 N. Mill St.
BARBER SHOPS
Mucklerogs, 617 N. Mill St.
SERVICE STATIONS
Johnson's, Kilgore & Tyler Hi'way
GARAGES
Holman's, Kilgore & Tyler Hi'way

HITCHCOCK

RESTAURANTS
Rose Bud, Hi'way 6
BARBER SHOPS
Fairwood, Hi'way 6
BEAUTY PARLORS
Mae's, Hi'way 6
SERVICE STATIONS
Brown's, Hi'way 6

HOUSTON

HOTELS
Crystal, 3308 Lyons Ave.
Y.M.C.A., 1217 Bagby St.
Cooper's, 1011 Dart St.
Ajapa, 2412 Dowling St.
New Day, 1912 Dowling St.
RESTAURANTS
Lincoln, Conti & Jenson
Lincoln, 2502 E. Alabama
Eva's, 1617 Dowling St.
CHINESE RESTAURANTS
Oriental, 2751 Lyons Ave.
TAVERNS
Black, 1808 Dowling St.
Welcome Cafe, 2409 Pease Ave.
Savoy No. 3321 Winbern
Potomic, 2721 Holman St.
BARBER SHOPS
Harris, 508 Louisiana St.
Grovey's, 2303 Dowling St.
Beau Brummel, 1512 Benson
BEAUTY PARLORS
School & Parlor, 222 W. Dallas
Lou Lillie's, 2108½ Jenson Dr.
Franklin, 2614 Dowling St.
NIGHT CLUBS
Club Matinee, 3224 Lyons Ave.
Bronze Peacock, 4104 Lyons
El Dorado, 2310 Elgin St.
Casino Club, 2004 Jensen Dr.
SERVICE STATIONS
Crystal White, 3222 Lyons Ave.
Lan's, 4312 Lyons Ave.
GARAGES
Jessie Jones, 1906 Dowling St.
Whiteside, 117 W. Dallas
TAXI CABS
Crystal, 3222 Lyons Ave.
DRUG STORES
Rolston, 3318 Lyons Ave.
Langford's, 3026 Pierce St.
Lion's, 618 Prarie & Louisiana
Eureka, 2322 Dowling St.
Forest Homes, 3033 Holman St.

MARSHALL

TOURIST HOME
Rev. Bailey, 1103 W. Grand Ave.
TAVERNS
Singleton, W. Grand Ave.
BARBER SHOPS
Craver's, So. Carter St.

MEXIA

HOTELS
Carleton, 1 W. Commerce St.
RESTAURANTS
Mrs. M. Carroll, 109 N. Belknap St.
BEAUTY PARLORS
Mrs. B. Smith, N. Denton
BARBER SHOPS
Mr. C. Carter, N. Belknap
TAVERNS
R. Houston, N. Belknap
NIGHT CLUBS
Payne's, West Side
ROAD HOUSES
Jim Ransom, N. Carthage
SERVICE STATIONS
Joe Brooks, 107 N. Belknap
GARAGES
Rev. T. Sparks, N. Belknap

MIDLAND

HOTELS
Watson's Hotel
RESTAURANTS
King Sandwich, 301 N. Lee
TAXI CABS
Johnnie's, 209 North Lee

PARIS

HOTELS
Brown Rigg, 322 N. E. 2nd St.
TOURIST HOMES
Mrs. I. Scott, 405 N. E. 2nd St.

PORT ARTHUR

RESTAURANTS
Shadowland, 632 W. 7th St.
Tick Tock, 536 W. 7th St.
BARBER SHOPS
Manhattan, 440 W. 7th St.
LIQUOR STORES
Messina's, 2147 Woodrow Dr.
Coleman's, 735 Texas Ave.

SAN ANTONIO

HOTELS
Manhattan, 735 E. Commerce
Nolan, 525 Nolan St.
Ross, 126 N. Mesquite St.
TOURIST HOMES
Mundy, 129 N. Mesquite St.
RESTAURANTS
Mamie's, 1833 E. Houston St.
Silver Slipper, 506 S. Gevers
BEAUTY SHOPS
Vessie's, 125 Canton St.
Jones, 209 N. Swiss St.
Optimistic, 105 Anderson St.
Band Box, 135 N. Mesquite St.
Mitts, 115 N. Swiss St.

Arritha's, 113 Alabama St.
R. & B., 126 N. Mesquite St.
Briscoe's, 515 S. Pine St.
Three Point, 716 Virginia Blvd.
Maggie Jones, 413 Center St.
NIGHT CLUBS
Wood Lake Country Club, New
Sulphur Spring Rd.
Key Hole, 1619 West Poplar
DRY CLEANING
C. L. Baho, 1843 E. Commerce St.
Dependable, 205 Losoya
Esquire, 212 Broadway
SERVICE STATIONS
Eason's, 1605 E. Houston St.
GARAGES
Eason's, 1606 E. Houston St.
DRUG STORES
W. H. Leonard, 701 S. Pine St.

TYLER

TOURIST HOMES
Mrs. Thomas, 516 N. Border St.
W. Langston, 1010 N. Border St.

TEXARKANA

RESTAURANTS
Casino, 504 West 3rd St.
GARAGES
Carl Hill's, 936 W. 20th St.

WACO

HOTELS
College View, 1129 Elm Ave.
TOURIST HOMES
B. Ashford, 902 N. 8th St.
BEAUTY PARLORS
Cendivilla, 107½ N. Second St.
Cinderella, 1133 Earle St.
Ideal, 1029 Taylor St.
Earle St., 1113 Earle St.
Mayfair, 112 Bridge St.
Modern, 1406 Taylor St.
Hine's, 1125 Earle St.
Murphy's, 115 So. 2nd St.
Odessa's, 920 Dawson St.
RESTAURANTS
Harlem, 123 Bridge
Ideal, 902 No. 8th St.
NIGHT CLUBS
Waco Loughorn, 19th & LaSalle
ROAD HOUSES
Golden Lilly, 426 Clifton
TAVERNS
Green Tree, 1325 S. 4th St.

WAXAHACHIE

TOURIST HOMES
Mrs. A. Nunn, 413 E. Main St.
Mrs. M. Johnson, 427 E. Main St.
Mrs. N. Lowe, 418 E. Main St.
Mrs. N. Jones, 430 E. Main St.

WICHITA FALLS

HOTELS
Bridges, 404 Sullivan St.
TOURIST HOMES
E. B. Jeffrey, 509 Juarez St.

UTAH

OGDEN

HOTELS
Royal, 2522 Wall Ave.

SALT LAKE CITY

HOTELS
Jenkin's Hotel
250 West South Temple
Sam Speed, 250 W. South Temple
Y.W.C.A., 306 E. 3rd St.
St. Louis Hotel
242½ West South Temple
Phone: 5-0838

VERMONT

BURLINGTON

HOTELS
The Pates, 86-90 Archibald St.
TOURIST HOMES
Mrs. William Sharper, 242 North St.

MANCHESTER

HOTELS
Clyde Blackwells

NORTHFIELD

TOURIST HOMES
Cole's Tourist Home, 7 Sherman
Ave.

RUTLAND

TOURIST HOMES
Mead Cottage, 24 High St.

VIRGINIA

ALEXANDRIA

TOURIST HOMES
J. T. Holmes, 803 Gibbon St.
J. A. Barrett, 724 Gibbon St.

BEDFORD

TOURIST HOMES
Marinda Jones, R. F. D. No. 1,
Box 7A

BRISTOL

TAVERNS
Morocco, 800 Spencer St.

BUCKROE BEACH

HOTELS
Bay Shore
NIGHT CLUBS
Club 400

CARET

TAVERNS
Sessons Tavern

CHARLOTTESVILLE

HOTELS
Carver Inn, 701 Preston Ave.
Paramount, West Main St.

TOURIST HOMES
Chauffeur's Rest, 129 Preston Ave.
Alexander's, 413 Dyce St.
BARBER SHOPS
Jokers, North 4th St.

CHRISTIANBURG

HOTELS
Eureka

COVINGTON

TOURIST HOMES
Mrs. Loretta S. Watson, 219
Lexington St.
RESTAURANTS
Silver Star, 208 So. Maple Ave.

CULPEPER

TOURIST HOMES
Maple Rest,
1018 South Main St.
Mrs. Mary L. Taylor, 1018 S. Main

DANVILLE

TOURIST HOMES
Mrs. P. M. Logan, 328 No. Main St.
Yancey's, 320 Holbrook St.
Mrs. M. K. Page, 434 Holbrook St.
Mrs. S. A. Overby, Holbrook St.
Mrs. Mary L. Wilson, 401 Holbrook
RESTAURANTS
Blue Room, 358 Holbrook St.

FARMVILLE

TOURIST HOMES
Mrs. K. Wiley, 626 Main St.
RESTAURANTS
Reid's, 236 Main St.
TAVERNS
Reid's, 200 Block, Main St.
SERVICE STATIONS
Clark's, Main St.

FREDERICKSBURG

HOTELS
McGuire, 521 Princess Anne St.
Rappahannock, 520 Princess St.
RESTAURANTS
Taylor's, 505 Princess Anne St.

HAMPTON

HOTELS
Savoy, 140 W. Queen St.
RESTAURANTS
Abraham's, 39th St. & Hi'Way
BARBER SHOPS
Paul's, 154 Queen St.
BEAUTY PARLORS
Tillie's, 215 N. King St.
SERVICE STATIONS
Lyle's, 40 Armitsead Ave.
GARAGES
Walton's, W. Mallory Ave.
TAXI CAB
Abraham's Taxi Service

66

HARRISONBURG

TOURIST HOME
Mrs. Ida M. Francis, 252 N. Main

HEWLETT

TAVERNS
Beverly Bros., R. F. D. No. 1

LEXINGTON

TOURIST HOMES
The Franklin, 9 Tucker St.
RESTAURANTS
Washington, 16 N. Main St.
TAVERNS
Rose Inn, 331 N. Main St.

LURAY

TOURIST HOMES
Camp Lewis Mountain, Skyline Dr.

LYNCHBURG

HOTELS
Hotel Douglas,
Route 29, North & South
Phone: 28841
Douglas, Rt. 29
Phyllis Wheatley Y.W.C.A., 613
Monroe St.
TOURIST HOMES
Mrs. C. Harper, 1109 8th St.
Mrs. N. P. Washington, 611 Polk
Mrs. Smith, 504 Jackson
Happyland Lake, 812 5th Ave.
BEAUTY PARLORS
Selma's, 1002 5th St.

NEWPORT NEWS

HOTELS
Cosmos Inn,
620 25th St.
TOURIST HOMES
Ritz, 636 25th St.
Mrs. W. E. Barron, 2123 Jefferson
Thomas E. Reese, 636 25th St.
Mrs. C. Stephens, 1909 Marshall
RESTAURANTS
Stop Light, 601 25th St.
Webb, 619 25th St.
BEAUTY PARLORS
Alice, 628 25th St.
SERVICE STATIONS
Ridley's, Orcutt Ave. & 36th St.
BARBER SHOPS
V. & R., 636 25th St.
TAILORS
Faulk, 638 25th St.
DRUG STORES
Woodard's, 25th St. & Madison

NORFOLK

HOTELS
Wheaton, 633 E. Brambleton Ave.
Tatum Inn, 453 Brewer St.
Plaza, 1757 Church St.
Y.M.C.A., 729 Washington Ave.
RESTAURANTS
Russell's, Grill, 816 Church St.
BEAUTY PARLORS
Jordan's, 526 Brambleton Ave.
Yeargen's, 1685 Church St.
Betty's, 641 E. Brambleton Ave.
Hazel, 363 E. Brambleton Ave.
DRUG STORES
Arthur's, 744 Church St.
Woods, 1000 Church St.
TAVERNS
Russell's, 835 Church St.
SERVICE STATION S
Alston's, Cor. 20th & Church St.

PETERSBURG

HOTELS
The Walker House, 116 South
NIGHT CLUBS
Chatter Boy, 143 Harrison St.

PHOEBUS

HOTELS
Horton's, County & Mellon Sts.
RESTAURANTS
Horton's, County & Mellon Sts.
DRUG STORES
Langley, County & Mellon Sts.
TAILORS
Perry, Mellon St.
SERVICE STATIONS
Ward's, County Nr. Fulton St.

RICHMOND

HOTELS
Slaughters, 529 N. 2nd St.
Harris, 200 E. Clay St.
Eggleston Miller's, 2nd & Leigh
TOURIST HOMES
Mrs. E. Brice, 14 W. Clay St.
Y.W.C.A., 515 N. 7th St.
BEAUTY PARLORS
Rest-a-Bit, 619 N. 3rd St.
BARBER SHOPS
Scotty's, 505 N. 2nd St.
TAVERNS
Market Inn, Washington Park
SERVICE STATIONS
Harris, 2205 Rockwood Ave.
Vaughn, 1701 Chamberlayne Ave.
Cameron's, Brook Ave. & W. Clay
Adam St., 523 N. Adam St.

ROANOKE
HOTELS
Dumas, Henry St. N. W.
TOURIST HOMES
Y.W.C.A., 205 2nd St. N. W.
DRUG STORES
Brook's, 221 N. Henry St.

COLVIN'S TOURIST HOME
All Modern Conveniences
Write or Phone for Reservations
Rate $3.00 and up
MRS. MARY B. COLVIN, Prop.
16 Gilmer Ave., N.W., Roanoke 17, Va.
Tel.: 2-3813

SOUTH HILL
HOTELS
Brown's, Melvin Brown, Prop.

STAUNTON
TOURIST HOMES
Pannell's Inn. 613 N. Augusta St.
RESTAURANTS
Johnson's, 301 N. Central Ave.

SUFFOLK
BEAUTY PARLORS
Lonely Hour Inn, Rt. 460

TAPPAHANNOCK
HOTELS
McGuire's Inn, Marsh St.
Mark, Haven Beach

WARRENTON
TOURIST HOMES
Lawson, 227 Alexander Pike
BARBER SHOPS
Walker's, 5th St
BEAUTY PARLORS
Fowlers, 123 N. 3rd St.
Pinn, 121 5th St.
TAXI CABS
Joyner's, Phone: 292
Bland, Phone: 430
Parker's, Phone: 491
TAILORS
McLain, 205 Culpepper St.

WILLIAMSBURG
HOTELS
Baker House, 419 Nicholson St.

WINCHESTER
HOTELS
Evans, 224 Sharp St.
RESTAURANTS
Ruth's, 128 E. Cecil St.
Dunbar Tea Room, 21 W. Hart St.

WASHINGTON
EVERETT
TOURIST HOMES
Mrs. J. T. Payne, 1632 Rainier St.
SEATTLE
HOTELS
Y.W.C.A., 709 29th Ave.
Atlas, 420 Maynard St.
Y.W.C.A., 709 29th Ave.
Green, 711 Lane St.
Idaho, 505 Jackson St.
Olympus, 413 Maynard St.
Eagle, 408½ Main St.
Mar, 520 Maynard Ave.
Welcome Annex, 613½ Jackson St.
TOURIST HOMES
Zora Rooms, 1826 23rd Ave.
M. Mathis, 1826 23rd Ave.
RESTAURANTS
Shanty Inn, 110 12th Ave.
Victory, 652 Jackson St.
BARBER SHOPS
Hayes, 2600 E. Valley St.
Stockards, 2632 E. Madison St.
Atlas, 410 Maynard Ave.
BEAUTY PARLOS
Catherine's, 410 Main St.
Pauline's, 2221 E. Madison
LaMode, 2039 E. Madison St.
Bert's, 2301 E. Denny Way
Glenarvons, 657 Jackson St.
NIGHT CLUBS
Playhouse, 1238 Main St.
LIQUOR STORES
Jackson's, 707 Jackson St.
TAVERNS
Mardi Gras, 2047 E. Madison St.
Hill Top, 1200 Jackson St.
Sea Gull, 673 Jackson St.
Lucky Hour, 1315 Yesler Way
Banquet, 1237 Jackson St.
Victory, 652 Jackson St.
Banquet, 1237 Jackson St.
Dumas, 1040 Jackson St.
GARAGES
Commercial Auto, 9th & Denny
DRUG STORES
Bon-Rot, 14th & Yesler St.
Bishop's, 567 Jackson St.
Chikata, 114 12th Ave.
Madison, 2051 E. Madison
Goshu, 656 Jackson St.
Tokuda, 1724 Yesler Way
Jackson St., Jackson & Maynard
TAILORS
Gilt Edge, 611 Jackson St.

TACOMA
HOTELS
Monte Carlo, 1555 Tacoma Ave.
RESTAURANTS
Monte Carlo, 1555 Tacoma Ave.
Travelers, 1506½ Pacific Ave.

WEST VIRGINIA

BECKLEY

HOTELS
New Pioneer, 340 S. Fayette
BEAUTY PARLORS
Katie's Vanity, S. Fayette
Fuqua's, Fuqua Bldg., S. Fayette
BARBER SHOPS
Payne's, 338 S. Fayette
Simpson's, New Pioneer Hotel
GARAGES
Moss's, 501 S. Fayette
DRUG STORES
Morton's, S. Fayette
TAXI CABS
Nuway, Dial 3301

BLUEFIELD

HOTELS
Travelers' Inn, 602 Raleigh St.
Hotel Thelma, 1047 Wayne St.
DRUG STORES
Kingslow's, Bland St.

CHARLESTON

HOTELS
Brown's, Capitol & Donnelly Sts.
Ferguson's, Washington St.
Penn's, West Charleston
RESTAURANTS
The Hut, 1329 Washington St.

SERVICE STATIONS
Bridge's Esso, Wash. & Truslow
TAXI CABS
Red Star, Dial 39-331

CHESTER

BARBER SHOPS
Kenneth B. Johnson, 505 Carolina

CLARKSBURG

LODGINGS
Mrs. Ruby Thomas, 309 Water St.
NIGHT CLUBS
American Legion, Monticello St.
Pythian, 119 Harper St.
Elks, First St.
TAVERNS
Johnson's, Monticello St.

FAIRMONT

HOTELS
Monongahela, Madison St.
RESTAURANTS
Whittaker's Grill, Pennsylvania
BEAUTY SCHOOLS
Parker's, Pennslyvania Ave.

GRAFTON

LODGINGS
Mrs. Geo. Jones, Front St.
RESTAURANTS
Jones'. Latrobe St.
TAVERNS
Boston's, 26 Latrobe St.

HINTON

HOTELS
The Price House,
109 9th Ave.
GUEST HOUSE
Maya's, State St.
DRY CLEANING
Emile's Cleaning & Pressing

HUNTINGTON

HOTELS
The Ross House, 911 8th Ave.
LODGINGS
Mrs. C. J. Barnett, 810 7th Ave.
RESTAURANTS
The Spot, 1614 8th Ave.
BEAUTY PARLORS
Louise's, Artisan Ave.
TAVERNS
Monroe's, 1616 8th Ave.
Finley's 8th & 16th
TAXI CABS
Party Taxi. Tel. 28385
SERVICE STATIONS
Sterling, Cor. 12th & 3rd

INSTITUTE

SERVICE STATIONS
White's Superette, Hi'Way 25
Pack's Esso

69

KEYSTONE
HOTELS
Franklin
DRUG STORES
Howard's Pharmacy
RESTAURANTS
Sam Wade's Cafe

KIMBALL
HOTELS
City Hotel
BEAUTY SHOPS
Smith's
RESTAURANTS
Palace

MONTGOMERY
HOTELS
New Royal, 223 Gaines St.
BEAUTY PARLORS
Snyder's, Fayette Pike
TAVERNS
The Green Front, 183½ 3rd Ave.
TAXI CABS
Gray's, 212 Gaines St.

MORGANTOWN
LODGINGS
Mrs. Linnie Mae Slaughter, 3 Cayton
Mrs. Jeannette O. Parker, 2 Cayton
NIGHT CLUBS
American Legion, University Pl.

MOUNDSVILLE
LODGINGS
Mrs. Blance Campbell, 1206 4th St.

NORTHFORK
HOTELS
Houchins Hotel & Cafe
BARBER SHOPS
Hough's

PARKERSBURG
NIGHT CLUBS
American Legion, 812 Avery St.

PRINCETON
TAVERNS
Twilight Inn, High St.
Spotlight Grill, Beckley Rd.

WEIRTON
LODGINGS
Mrs. Robert Williams, Kessel St.

WELCH
HOTELS
Capehart, 14 Virginia Ave.

WHEELING
HOTELS
Blue Triangle, Y.W.C.A.
108 12th St.
Verse, 1042 Market St.
LODGINGS
Mrs. W. C. Turner, 114 12th St.

RESTAURANTS
Blue Goose, 1035 Chapline St.
BEAUTY PARLORS
Mode-Craft, 1028½ Chapline St.
NIGHT CLUBS
American Legion, 1045 Chapline
Elk's Club, 1005½ Chapline St.
DRUG STORES
North Side Pharmacy, Chapline St.

WHITE SULPHUR SPRINGS
LODGINGS
Brooks, 138 Church St.
Haywood Place, Church St.
Slaughter's, Tel. 9280

WILLIAMSON
LODGINGS
Mrs. A. Wright, 605 Logan St.
DRUG STORES
Whittico's
NIGHT CLUBS
Elk's Club, Vinson St.
TAILOR SHOPS
Garner's, Logan St.

WISCONSIN

FOND DU LAC
TOURIST HOMES
Mrs. E. Pirtle, 45 E. 11th St.
V. Williams, 97 S. Seymour St.

MILWAUKEE
HOTELS
Hillcrest Hotel
504 W. Galena St.
ROOMING HOUSES
Mrs. Nettie M. Brown
920 W. Wright St.
Phone: Franklin 4-1965
Pastell Lampkins, 2427 N. 14th St.
Mrs. Margaret Burns
1241 North 6th St.
Johnson's Rooms
1033 W. Somers St.
Mrs. Sally King
2328 West 12th St.

RESTAURANTS
North Side, 2141 N. 16th St.
Black King, 1342 N. 5th St.
Larry's, 619 W. Walnut St.
Carl's Ideal Eat Shoppe
628 W. Juneau Ave.
Christine's, 614 W. Juneau
Hargroves, 1443 N. 3rd St.
Barnes, 409 W. Brown St.
Hickory, 1243 W. McKinley St.
Kiner, 1457 N. 7th St.
Sun Flower, 500 W. Vine St.
Boatner's, 709 W. Walnut St.

Knights Restaurant
1501 North 7th St.
Moseby's, 1602 N. 7th St.

Our Chicken Shack
537 W. Walnut St.
Huff 7 Puff, 1504 W. Juneau
Gay Paree, Cor. 7th & Galena Sts.

Eddie's Restaurant
504 W. Galena St.

BARBER SHOPS
Hollywood, 2676 N. 5th St.
Handsome, 828 W. Walnut St.
Veterans, 1017 W. Walnut St.
Matthew's, 800 W. Lloyd St.
Peoples, 504 W. Juneau Ave.
Colonial, 610 W. Walnut St.
Corley's, 903 W. Walnut St.
De Luxe, 939 W. Walnut St.
Rainbow, 1646 N. 6th St.
Sterling, 837 W. Walnut St.
William's, 531 W. Walnut St.

BEAUTY PARLORS
Poro, 1820 N. 7th St.
House of Beauty, 822 W. N. Ave.
Rosa Lee, 2245 North 6th St.
Victory, 1426 West N. Ave.
Blanche's, 726 West Walnut St.
Enchanted, 815 W. North Ave.
Apex, 2101 North 7th St.
Augusta's, 1649 North 10th St.
Freddie's, 1820 North 6th St.
Little's, 625 West Walnut St.
Moderne, 1909 N. 12th St.
Novelty, 965 W. Walnut St.
Sally's, 1116 W. Walnut St.
Vogue, 923 W. Walnut St.
Unique, 717 W. Somers St.

TAVERNS
Midway Inn,
1000 W. Galena St.
Vine Street Tavern
341 West Vine St.
Lucille's, 2052 N. 7th St.
Liberty, 1745 N. 3rd St.
Tally-Ho, 600 W. Lloyd St.
Fat's, 1810 N. 3rd St.
Bronze Bar, 1239 N. 6th St.
Jon & Lou's, 823 W. Walnut St.
High Step, 908 W. Galena
Star, 2479 N. 8th St.
Thelma's, 701 W. Juneau Ave.

TIP TOP TAVERN
WE HAVE ALL POPULAR BRANDS
Meals & Sandwiches Served
1800 N. 10th St., Milwaukee 5, Wisc.
Tel.: Concord 9819

Curley's, 1744 N. 3rd St.
Butch's, 1008 W. Somers St.
Andy's, 1748 N. 7th St.
Floyd's, 1222 N. 7th St.
Cork & Bottle, 1601 N. 12th St.
Nino's, 1111 W. Vliet St.
Gold Coast, 638 W. Walnut St.
Knox's, 608 W. Walnut St.
Milt's, 1039 W. Walnut St.

NIGHT CLUBS
Flame, 1315 N. 9th St.

CHINESE RESTAURANTS
Loy's, 705 W. Juneau Ave.

LIQUOR STORES
Wisconsin House, 336 W. Walnut

DRUG STORES
Dr. Edgar Thomas
440 W. Galena St.
Community, 440 W. Galena St.
Neighborhood, 1802 N. 7th St.
Lloyd's, 725 W. Walnut St.
Shaw's, 1701 W. State St.
Schroeder, 1951 N. 3rd St.

TAILORS
Helens, 1249 N. 7th St.
Hiawatha, 512 W. Center St.

Wilcher's Tailoring Shop
1830 North 12th St.
Comet, 916 W. North Ave.

W. A. Mason,
732 W. Walnut St.
General, 2018 N. 10th St.
Ideal, 214 W. Wells St.

SERVICE STATIONS
Paul's, 200 No. 8th St.
Paul Schraven, 12th & Garfield
Abbott's, 1319 W. North Ave.
Park's, 1616 N. 7th St.
Gary's, No. 11th & W. Vliet Sts.
Derby's, 603 W. Walnut St.
Huff & Barker, 539 W. Cherry St.
Tankar, 735 W. Walnut St.

GARAGES
Adolph's, 1625 A North 9th St.
A. & E., 759A W. Winnebago St.
Community, 1920 N. 9th St.
McGee's, 624 W. Juneau Ave.
St. Paul, 1218 N. 7th St.
Universal, 2244 N. 34th St.
T. & H., 1218 N. 7th St.

GROCERY STORES
Patterson's Grocery
2109 North 6th St.
Triangle Market
1767 North 7th St.
Rhodes Grocery
901 W. Galena St.
Keene's Grocery
1953 North 8th St.

TAXI CABS
Apex Amusement
819 W. Walnut St.
HABERDASHERY
Matherson Haberdashery
623 W. Walnut St.
PHOTOGRAPHER
Hillside Photographic Studio
1243 A North 7th St.
UNDERTAKER
Raynor & Reed, 1816 N. 7th St

BELOIT
BARBER SHOPS
Hobson's, 441 St. Paul
RESTAURANTS
Hobson's, 102 Park Ave.
SERVICE STATIONS
Collins, Colby St.
TAVERNS
Clover Leaf, 163 Prospect

MADISON
RESTAURANTS
Twilight, 838 W. Washington
BEAUTY PARLORS
Emily's, 16 So. Murray
TAILORS
Guy's, 316 E. Main St.

RACINE
RESTAURANTS
Hadley's, 2121½ Meade St.

OSHKOSH
TOURIST HOMES
F. Pemberton, 239 Liberty St.

WYOMING

CASPER
TOURIST HOMES
Mrs. David J. Rudd, 646 E. "A" St.

RAWLINGS
RESTAURANTS
Yellow Front, 11 E. Front St.
TOURIST HOMES
Hobert Westbrook, 111 E. Front St.

ROCK SPRINGS
TOURIST HOMES
Collins Tourist Home, 915 7th St.

ALASKA

FAIRBANKS
HOTELS
Savoy

Please Mention the "Green Book"

in Patronizing These Places

Bermuda

Out in the Mid-Atlantic, south east of the Virginia Capes, beyond the Gulf Stream's flying fish and phosphorous, lie the most famous coral islands in the World. It is the Bermudas . . . less than 20 square miles in size and so formed that in few spots it is possible to get more than a mile away from the sea. The north and south shores are utterly different and might belong to countries hundreds of leagues apart.

The Bermudas, with startling clarity of sunlight, their gentle tropical sea, their special flash of white washed roofs, pink-tinted walls and flaming poinciana trees, and their island nights glittering with more stars than any other sky in the Atlantic. They are collectively called "Bermuda." Here we find a place of coveted ease, unhurried charm and relaxed living.

Here it may mean building castles in the cleanest pink and white sand on earth, wandering over coral beaches into ocean that is the greenest green, the bluest blue. It may mean cycling along South Shore Road between tall hedges of Oleander, with youngster and picnic lunches safely tucked in a basket on handle bars.

Or it may be the velvety greens and fairways of one of Bermuda's many golf courses. Or where attractive shops show choicest merchandise of the British Empire.

There are many beautifully kept tennis courts, hidden picnic beaches, delightful roads and coral rocks from which a native fisherman's net may be cast, ensnaring everything including prancing, sea-horses and mermaids singing! For, like a jewel set in Mid-Atlantic, Bermuda is the wish at sunset and romance is starlight.

HOW DO I GET TO BERMUDA?

You go from one Parish to another by boat, by bicycle, by the small motor car. Everywhere the place is leisurely. The motor car convenient for visits from one end of the islands to the other, travels (by law) only a few miles faster than average horse and carriage.

You fly by the latest aircraft or

St. Peter's Church, St. Georges

73

you go by luxury liner. The plane takes a few hours, boats from New York, 35 hours. Departures from Baltimore, Boston, Halifax, Montreal and England. When you make reservations inquire about special rates for children

CURRENCY

Although sterling is the legal tender in Bermuda, American and Canadian currencies are accepted everywhere. United Kingdom Bank Notes are still not negotiable.

FACTS ABOUT BERMUDA

Entry Requirements—No one requires passports or visas for visits to Bermuda, for periods of less than eight months. United States citizens require same form of identification and proof of citizenship when returning to the U. S. A.

THINGS TO SEE IN BERMUDA

Somerset Tour — One day, Ferry from Hamilton to Somerset Island, returning by taxi, carriage or bicycle. Several interesting places in Somerset for lunch. See unique Somerset Bridge, visit U. S. Naval Base, enjoy panorama of Bermuda from gallery of Gibbs Hill Lighthouse.

ST. GEORGES TOUR— ONE DAY

Because of long journey to the town of St. George, you will have more time to see if you go by taxi. Points of especial interest in St. George, St. Peter's Church, the old United States House, St. George's Historical Museum, Gates Fort and David's Lighthouse.

TEMPERATURE

Mild and Equable, never far off 70.7. No sudden changes occur. Rainfall brief and skies clear very quickly after a shower.

WHAT TO WEAR

During warmer months (mid-March to mid-November) cotton dresses and afternoon dress, a long one for evening, summer sportsclothes. For Men — Light weight suits, sport clothes, Bermuda shorts, white dinner jackets. During cooler months (mid-November to mid-March) light wool dresses, sweaters and skirts, warm suit, dinner dresses, top coat. For Men — tweed jacket, slacks, tweed or flannel suits, sportswear, afternoon clothes, sweaters, dinner jacket, top coat.

Queen Street, St. Georges, Bermuda

74

BERMUDA

ST. GEORGES
GUEST HOUSE
"Archlyn Villa," Wellington St.
LIQUOR STORE
Packwood's, Walter St.
BICYCLES
Dowling's Cycle Livery, York St.

PENBROKE
HOTELS
Richmond House, Richmond Rd.
GUEST HOUSE
Milestone, Coxs Hill

W. PEMBROKE
GUEST HOUSE
Sunset Lodge, P. O. Box 413

WARRICK
GUEST HOUSE
Mrs. Leon Eve, Snake Rd.
Homeleigh, Mrs. D. Eave, Prop.
Hilton Manor, Mrs. W. Tucker, Prop.

HAMILTON
HOTELS
Imperial, Church St.
GUEST HOUSES
Ripleigh, Mrs. Doris Pearman,
RESTAURANTS
Blue Jay, Church St.
The Spot, Burnaby St.

CANADA

COLLINGWOOD
TOURIST HOMES
Cedar Inn, P. O. Box 265
MONTREAL
TOURIST HOMES
Mrs. Cummings, 764 Atwater Ave.
Davis, 1324 Torrence St.
Mrs. N. P. Morse, 932 Calumet Pl.
Au Repos Rooms
1824 Dorchester St., West.
BEAUTY PARLORS
Mendes, 2036 St. Antoine St.

CARIBBEAN

BARBADOES, St. Michael
GUEST HOUSES
West Gate, West Gate, Landsend
ST. JOHN'S, ANTIGUA
American House, Redcliff St.
PORT-AU-PRINCE, HAITI
Beau Site, Frank Cardozo, rPop.
NASSAU, BAHAMAS
Shalimar, P. O. Box 606

MEXICO

ENSENADS
MOTELS
James Littlejohn, Highway 101
MONTERREY
HOTELS
Hotel Genova, Madero Blvd.
RESTAURANT
El Tapinumba
JACALA
TOURIST HOMES
Pemex
TAMAZUNCHALE
TOURIST HOMES
Pemex
IXQUIMILIPAN
TOURIST HOMES
Pemex
CUERNAVACA
TOURIST HOME
Butch's Manhattan, on the Hi'way
MEXICO CITY
HOTELS
Hotel Carlton, Ignacia Marisca
NIGHT CLUB
The Waikiki, Paseo de la Reforma

SAN JOSE,
COSTA RICA,
CENTRAL AMERICA

HOTELS
Castilla, Calle 6, Ave. 1/3
Continental, Calle 3, Ave. 3/5
Europa, Calle Av., Ave. 5
Latimo, Calle 6, Ave. 3
Pan American, CS. 3/5, Ave. F. G.
Rex, Calle 2, Ave. F.G./2
Anexo, CS. 7/9, Ave. F.G.
Central, Calle 6, Ave. 2
Costa Rica, Calle 3, Aves. F.G/2
Las Americas, Calle 8, Ave. 3/5
Metropoli, CS. 1/3, Ave. F.G.
Regina, Calle 5, Ave. 3
Ritz, Calle 11, Ave. 3
Trebol, CS. 8/9, Ave. 3
RESTAURANTS
El Torino, Calle 6, Ave. 5
La Eureka, CS. 4/6, A.F.G.
El Imperio, Calle 6/8, Ave. 3
El Nido, Calle 6, Ave. 1/3
Roma, Calle 3, Ave. 1
El Moderino, Calle 2, Ave. 6
La Esmeralda, C. Av., F.G./2
La nava, Calle 9, Avs. 12/14
Tavernsperial, Calle 6, Ave. 2

THE GREEN BOOK VACATION GUIDE

Introduction . . .

To assist you in planning your vacation, to help you make it a better and a more enjoyable holiday than it has ever been, this section is dedicated.

Choose the Vacation which most perfectly matches your mood and pocketbook. By listing the names and addresses of the various resorts, it is easy to write and secure your reservations. Where no address is supplied, write to the city mentioned during the summer months.

This year make it a grand and glorious vacation and use this booklet to help you to decide where you would like to go.

Our Vacation Reservation Serv-ice will be ready each year to make your reservation from the places advertised.

Our advertisers are ready and willing to give you the best there is, to make you comfortable — to see to it that you have an enjoyable time, so that you may return from your vacation feeling fit for your job.

To select the perfect place in which to spend your vacation, and to get the most out of your stay, it is suggested that you:

Select the state that you wish most to visit.

Make y o u r reservations far enough in advance through VICTOR H. GREEN & Co. to be sure that you can be accommodated.

COLORADO

PINE CLIFF
Wink's Panorama Lodge

CONNECTICUT

WEST HAVEN
Dadd's Hotel, 359 Beach St.
Sea View Hotel, 39? Beach St.
Home of Hawkins. 372 Beach St.

DELAWARE

MILLSBORO
Rosedale Beach
FRANKFORD
Briarwood Farm
REHOBOTH BEACH
Mallory Cabins, Mrs. Mary
E. Mallory

FLORIDA

FERNANDINA
Hotel American Beach, P. O.
Box 195

M A I N E

OGUNQUIT
Viewland
Mace Guest House, 20 Agamenticus

GARDINER
Pond View. R.F.D. 1*A

FAYETTE
Pine Cone Lodge, P. O. Box 12

NORCROSS POND
Lodge Norcross

WEST SCARBOROUGH
Elcla Acres
Spring Hill Farm, R. F. D. 1

SACO
Coley Acres, Portland St.

WELLINGTON
Picturesque Manor
Mrs. E. E. Walker
743 Chestnut St. Camden 3, N. J.

76

MARYLAND

ANNAPOLIS
  Carr's Beach
  Sparrow's Point, P. O. Box 266
BENEDICT
  Violet Belles Hotel
COLTON
  Shirley K Hotel
WESTMINSTER
  Scarletts Country Club

INDIANA

ANGOLA
  Pryor's Country Place, R. R. No. 2

MASSACHUSETTS

FALMOUTH
  La Casa Linda, Indiana Ave.
FRANKLIN
  The Franklin House, 509 Maple St.
OSTERVILLE
  The Roost, P. O. Box 488
OAK BLUFFS
  Brownies Cottage, P. O. Box 788
  The Eastman's, P. O. Box 1221
HYANNISPORT
  Dr. M. C. Tohmpson, 181 Windsor
  Hilltop, P. O. Box 205
BILLERICA
  Galehurst, P. O. Box 583
CANTON
  Peter Pan House, 808 West St.
  Whispering Willow, 808 West St.
EAST BROOKFIELD
  Camp Atwater
KINGSTON
  Camp Twin Oaks
  Kingston Inn
MASHPEE
  Camp Maushop, P. O. Box 7
  The Guest House, P. O. Box 234
NORWELL
  Norwell Pines, P. O. Box 234
OAK BLUFFS
The O'Brien House
220-222 Circuit Ave.
  Shearer Cottage
  Scott's Cottage, P. O. Box 1121
  Maxwell Cottage, P. O. Box 1354
  Lill & Delta Cottage, School St.
VINEYARD HAVEN
  Araujo Rooms, P. O. Box 518
WAREHAM
  Clipper Cabins, 294 Elm St.
  Stockbridge, Mass.
  Parkview, Park St.
WEST HYANNIS
  West Hyannis Port, Craryville Rd.
WILLIAMSTOWN
  Hart's Camp

MINNESOTA

PINE RIVER
  Ware's Resort, 50 Lakes Rt.
BACKUS
  Pine Mt. Camp

NEW YORK STATE

ACCORD
  Rock Hill Farm Camp
ALLABEN
  Camp Bryton Rock
ATHENS
  Riverview, R. F. D. 1
BLOOMINGBURG
  Harper's Lodge
CATSKILL
  Camp Sky Mountain, R. F. D. 1.
    Box 195
  Johnson's Inn, Cauterskill Ave.
CHESTERTON
  Crystal Lake Lodge
CLINTON CORNERS
  The Patches, Jameson Hill Rd.
CUDDEBACKVILLE
  Paradise Farm
EDDIEVILLE
  Boston Terrace
  Arrow Lodge
GREENWOOD LAKE
  La Part Cabins in the Sky
  Just Haven
  Mrs. Louise Taylor, P. O. Box 314
  Farm Lake House
GLEN FALLS
  McFerson's Hotel, 52 Glen St.
GLENWILD
  Camp Napretep
HUNTER
  Notch Mountain House P. O.
    Box 5
HIGH FALLS
  Clove Valley Dude Ranch
HOLMES
  Lake Drew Lodge, 100 W. 138th St.
ROSENDALE
  Rosendale Gardens, P. O. Box 154
  Jumping Hooster Country Club
STUYVESANT
  Simmons Farm
NAPANOCH
  Shangri-La Country Club
KINGSTON
  Lang's Ranch, Route 4, Box 302
HIGH FALLS
  Wickie Wackie Club
STONE RIDGE
  Hy Charles Farm, Box 303
WEST BROOKVILLE
  Glen Terrace Hotel
WARWICK
  Appalachian Lodge, R. D. 1,
    Box 33
  Lakeland

KERHONKSON
Rainbow Acres
KINGSTON
Moulton's Retreat, R. F. D. 4,
Box 251
LAKE GEORGE
Woodbine Cottage, 75 Dieskau St.
LAKE PLACID
Dreamland Cottage, 41 Mckinley St.
Camp Parkside, Woodland Terrace
LIVINGSTON MANOR
Hillside Camp
MECHANICVILLE
Comfort Inn, R. F. D. 1
MONROE
Lakeside Farm
Mrs. Lottie Henderson, R. F. D. 1
Randolph's Mt. Lake Lodge
R. F. D. 1, Box 198
MONTGOMERY
Sumphaven Lodge, R. F. D. New Rd
OTISVILLE
King's Lodge
Mountainside Farm, P. O. Box 207
NEW YORK CITY, N. Y.
Brucewood, 321 W. 125th St.
PLEASANT VALLEY
Brown Hill Farm, R. F. D. 1
RIFTON
Maple Tree Inn, P. O. Box 116
ROXBURY
New Mt. Viek House, P. O. Box 120
SARATOGA SPRINGS
Nimmo Manor, 21 Federal St.
Richards, 29 Ballston Ave.
Jemmott's Inn, 22 Cowen St.
Branchcomb Cottage, 18 Cherry St.
James' Guest House, 17 Park St.
STAATSBURG
White Wall Manor
STORMVILLE
Mountain View Farm, R. F. D. 16
The Cecil Lodge, R. F. D.
SPRING VALLEY
White Birches, S. Pascack Rd.
WINGDALE
Camp Unity
WHITE LAKE
Fur Workers Resort
VERBANK
Sunset Hill Farm
VALLEY COTTAGE
Mtn. View Lodge, Mt. View Ave.

LONG ISLAND
AMITYVILLE
Van Winn Villa, Albany Ave.
& Reed Rd.
DEER PARK
Deer Haven, 1531 Deer Park Ave.
EAST MEREDITH
Stone House, Mrs. C. B. Simkins,
GREENPORT
Sea Breeze Cottage, 321 7th St.
R. F. D.

MEDFORD
Gordon Hgts. Rest
Flor's Cottage, P. O. Box 211
HAMMELS
The Cherokee, 217 Beach 76th St.
JAMAICA
Lillie's Cottage, 147-11 Ferndale
PATCHOGUE
Martin Acres, Yaphank Rd.
QUOGUE
Shinnecock Arms, Jessup Ave.
Williams Cottage
Arch Cottage, P. O. Box 761
ROCKAWAY BEACH
Regina House, 223 Beach 77th St.
Ocean View, 232 Beach 77th St.
The Cherokee, 217 Beach 76th St.
SAG HARBOR
Douglas Cottage
SOUTHOLD
Cherry-Wells Brung., P. O. Box 571
SOUTHAMPTON
Starlight Rest, 111 Pelletreau St.
Kellis Rest, P. O. Box 112
Ross Acres, Box 536

NEW JERSEY

ATLANTIC CITY
Jones Cottage, 1720 Arctic Ave.
Apex Rest, Indiana & Ontario Aves
Wright's Hotel, 1702 Arctic Ave.
Gregory Frances House, 232
N. Virginia Ave.
ASBURY PARK
Wright's Cottage, 153 Sylan Ave.
Ada's Cottage, 1404 Sumerfield
Gladstone Cottage, 1701 Bangs Ave.
Hotel Carver, 312 Myrtle Ave.
Rhine Cliff Cottage, 138 Reage Ave.
BELMAR
Pleasant View House, 504 11th Ave.
LaPetite Cottage, 502 16th Ave.
Baldwin Cottage, 610 11th Ave.
Riverview Inn, 710 8th Ave.
Sadie's Guest House, 1304 E. St.
CAPE MAY
Stiles, 821 Corgie St.
CLIFFWOOD
Forbes Beach, P. O. Box 231
FARMINGDALE
Mrs. N. Perry, R. F. D. No. 1,
Box 400
Blue Top Cottage, Shark River Rd.
LONG BRANCH
Albreco Anchorage, 395 Atlantic
LONG BRANCH, West End
Metropolitan Seashore Home,
8 Cottage Ave.
MAHWAH
Josie Rue Acres, P. O. Box 184
OCEAN CITY
Hotel Comfort, 201 Bay Ave.
Bryson's, 6th & Simpson Ave.

NEPTUNE
Busy Bee Cottage, 446 Fisher Ave.
Shore Villa, 316 Myrtle Ave.
MILLINGTON
Playland Farms
MIDVALE
Camp Midval
NORTH LONG BRANCH
Shady Nook Cot., 71 Atlantic Ave.
LAKEHURST
Robertson's Farm
NEW GRENTA
Oaklawn Country Club
PLEASANTVILLE
Morris Beach, 401 Bayview Ave.
Garden Spot, 300 Doughty Rd
Marionette Cottage, 604 Portland
RICHLAND
Red Oaks Rest
SKILLMAN
Rainbow End
SPRINGLAKE BEACH
Laster Cottage, 419 Morris Ave.
TOMS RIVER
McDaniel Farm, 2 Rover Rd.
WILDWOOD
Poindexter Cottage,
166 E. Schellenger Ave.
Mrs. J. B. Quarles, 100 Young Ave.

MICHIGAN

BALDWIN
Whip-or-Will Cot. Rt. 1,
Box 178B
Three Sisters
CONSTANTINE
Double J. Ranch, Jean S. Jones,
BAY SHORE
Zac White Pines
BUCHANAN
Waters Farm
BITLEY (Woodland Park Resort
Old Dears Rest, Rt. 1
Dagg's Cottage, Rt. 1
Everett Rest Haven, Rt. 1
Royal Breeez Hotel, Rt. 1
Caslea's Blue Bell Garden, Rt. 1
COVERT
Scott's, Country Villa, Rt. 1, Box 53
Pitchford's, Big Tower Child.
Camp. Tel. OA 4-4749
Mable's Place
HART
Bryson's, on the Hilltop
202 N. State St.
HARTFORD
Matthew Burgess' Place
IDLEWILD

The Pomiserania Lodge
Mildred Williams
Club El Morocco, Rt. 1, Box 186A
Bask-Inn, Broadway & Hemlock
Douglas Manor, P. O. Box 794
McKnight's Par. Pal., P. O. Box 75

White Way Inn, Broadway
Lydia Inn, P. O. Box 81
Rosana Tavern, Lake Drive
Nichol's Home, P. O. Box "B"
Morton's Motel, P. O. Box 116
LAWRENCE
FloraGiles Farm, Rt. 1
PAW PAW

Trails End Resort
Pit's Resort, Rt. 1, Box 131
ROSE CENTER
Medicine Acres, 8775 Water St.
SOUTH HAVEN
Thornton's Resort, Rt. 3, Box 41
Johnson's Shady Nook, Rt. 1,
Box 102
Twin Star Resort, Rt. 3, Box 245
Clare Harris' Resort, Rt. 4, Box 38
Evergreen Resort
THREE RIVERS
Wilson's Farm, Rt. 2, Box 344
Jordan's Home, Rt. 2, Box 546
VANDALIA (Paradise Lk. Resort
Three Sisters, Rt. 1

PENNSYLVANIA

STROUDSBURG
Stroudsburg Mt. View House,
14 No. 2nd St.
EAST STROUDSBURG
Fern Board. House, 387 Lincoln
ESPY
Sunrise, P. O. Box 65
MONROETON
Dorsey Wood Park Farm,
R. F. D. 1
MT. POCONO
The Carter House, 15 Quay St.
SWIFTWATER
Alenia's Inn, Box 236
WILLOW GROVE
Laster Chateau, 428 S. Easton Rd.

79

RHODE ISLAND

WESTERLY
Orchard House

SOUTH CAROLINA

OCEAN DRIVE
Atlantic Beach
Hotel Gordon, Atlantic Beach

VERMONT

MANCHESTER
Limberlock

NORTHFIELD
Cole's Brown Bung. 7 Sherman Ave.

VIRGINIA

CROZET
Mtn. View Farm. R. F. D. 1,
Box 52

ORANGE
Mrs. B. Wood, R. F. D. 2

BEDFORD
Mrs. M. Jones, R. F. D. 1, Box 7A

CATAWBA
Mrs. E. Sorano, R. F. D. 1,
Box 32A

LYNNHAVEN
Ocean Breeze Beach
TAPPAHANNOCK
Mark-Haven Beach

WISCONSIN

FORT ATKINSON, WISCONSIN

BURNS' RESORT

House-Keeping Cabins
Good Fishing, Boats & Bait
For Reservations write:
Rt. 3, Box 266   Phone: 850-J-2

SPOONER
Lone Star Resort, Rt. 2
Channey's Resort, Rt. 2

TOMAHAWK
Somom Heights Resort

CANADA

COLLINGWOOD (ONTARIO)
Cedar Inn, P. O. Box 265
SHEFFIELD'S CEDAR INN
P. O. BOX 265
MUSKOKA
Black & Tan Resort
QUEBEC
Husband's Resort, 6 Calixa
MONTREAL
TOURIST HOMES
Mrs. N. P. Morse, 922 Calumet Pl.
Mrs. A. Cummines, 764 Atwater
Davis Home, 1324 Torrence St.
AuRepos Rooms, 1824 Dorchester
Grant House, 1432 St. Antoine St.

THIS GUIDE

is Consulted

Throughout

the Year

by

Thousands

of

Travelers

Are You

Represented?

FREE

to your friends...
a copy of The

GREEN BOOK

*Want to show them
what a valuable
guide this is and
why you order
same?*

You can send a FREE
sample copy to as many
friends as you like. Just
give their names and
addresses and we'll do
the rest—at no cost to
you or your friends.
Of course, we will send
it to them with your
compliments and ours.

❧

VICTOR H. GREEN
& CO.
Publishers
200 West 135th Street
New York 30, N. Y.

History

The Green Book, first published in 1936 under the title *The Negro Motorist Green Book*, was a product of the rising African-American middle class having the finances and vehicle for travel but facing a world where social and legal resirictions barred them from many accomodations. At the time, there were thousands of "sundown towns", towns where African Americans were legally barred from spending the night there at all.

The book provided a guide to hotels and restaurant that would accept their business, often ones established specifically for the black customer. Published annually by Victor Hugo Green, a New Yorker who retired from his work as a mailman based on its success and expanded into the travel reservation business, the Green Book was for decades a vital handbook, fading out of business only after the civil rights laws of the 1960s brought about the end of legal segregation. It was sold largely through mail order

Victor H. Green
1892 – 1960

and through service stations - specifically, through Esso stations, as Esso not only served African-American customers, they were willing to franchise their stations to African-Americans, unlike most petroleum companies of the day. The guide was also offered by AAA and distributed elsewhere with advice from the United States Travel Bureau, a government agency

Also available:
THE 1940 EDITION!

Recommended Readings

- The Teachings of Ptahhotep: The Oldest Book in the World

- The Five Negro Presidents: According to what White People Said They Were

- 100 Amazing Facts About the Negro with Complete Proof: A Short Cut to The World History of The Negro

- From Babylon to Timbuktu: A History of the Ancient Black Races Including the Black Hebrews

Available at www.snowballpublishing.com

Printed in the USA
CPSIA information can be obtained
at www.ICGtesting.com
LVHW051604221123
764524LV00002B/13

9 781684 117079